Regulation Without the State ... The Debate Continues

John Blundell
Colin Robinson

With Commentaries by
Norman Barry
David Boaz
Christopher Fildes
Lord Haskins
Randall S. Kroszner
Graeme Leach
Yesim Yilmaz

And a Foreword by
Martin Ricketts

Published by The Institute of Economic Affairs 2000

First published in September 2000 by
The Institute of Economic Affairs
2 Lord North Street
Westminster
London SW1P 3LB

IEA Readings 52
All rights reserved
ISSN 0305-814X
ISBN 0 255 36483-0

Printed in Great Britain by
Hartington Fine Arts Limited, Lancing, West Sussex
Set in Times Roman 11 on 13 point

Contents

Introduction

IN JULY 1999, WE PUBLISHED *Regulation Without the State* (IEA Occasional Paper 109). We received many comments on the paper, from readers in Britain and outside, most of which supported our view that government regulation has become excessive and has crowded out private forms of regulation. An indication of how widespread is concern about government regulation is the number of requests which have been received to translate *Regulation Without the State*: Spanish and Portuguese editions have already appeared.

For three reasons we concluded that the Institute should provide a forum for further debate about regulation. *First* is the interest the paper has aroused. *Second* is the increasing volume of media comment on regulation which reinforces our view that this is one of the big issues of our time for business and consumers which requires serious analysis. *Third* is the detectable change of emphasis in official and semi-official documents[1] which now point out the advantages of 'self-regulation' – which was one of the principal themes of our paper. Rather than simply reprinting a second impression, it therefore seemed desirable to seek out and air other views on the topic.

Consequently, we invited a number of people who have thought and written about regulation to contribute to a successor volume. The result is Readings 52 in which the original version of *Regulation Without the State* is reprinted with seven commentaries.

The first commentary, by **Professor Norman Barry** of the University of Buckingham, takes a critical look at regulations as 'devices for hampering, if not completely disabling, the private enterprise system'. Professor Barry would like to introduce competition between regulatory regimes in decentralised political units, giving citizens the power of exit from regimes they do not like.

David Boaz, Executive Vice President of the Cato Institute in Washington, DC, then gives some specific examples of private regulation, describing the benefits of branding to consumers, explaining how private insurance performs a regulatory role and showing how

---

[1] For example, Better Regulation Task Force, *Self-Regulation Interim Report*, October 1999.

private communities (including shopping malls) create safety and stability.

Christopher Fildes, the distinguished columnist of the *Daily Telegraph* and the *Spectator*, contributes a topical regulatory tale about financial services. The tale ends with a one-clause Bill passing through Parliament which says the law governing the sale of goods should be taken as applying to financial services.

Lord Haskins, Chairman of the UK government's Better Regulation Task Force, stresses that his Task Force is '… keen, where possible, to find solutions to problems without resorting to state regulation' and also points to insurance as an '… effective alternative to state regulation'. He sees virtues in self-regulation, even though he thinks it is not satisfactory in all cases.

Professor Randall Kroszner, of the University of Chicago School of Business, argues that growth in international financial markets has been stimulated by '… the avoidance of traditional government regulation.' Market forces have, he claims, created order out of the '… apparent chaos of the international banking and financial markets'.

Graeme Leach, Chief Economist of the Institute of Directors, contends that the regulatory burden in the UK has risen under the present government: the direct and indirect costs could now amount to 9% of UK GDP. Moreover, there is a serious 'regulatory threat' from the European Union.

In the final commentary, **Yesim Yilmaz**, who is a PhD candidate at George Mason University, Fairfax, Virginia, finds the case for safety and quality regulation by the state to be weak. She explains how market-based institutions deal with quality and safety in ways which are both low-cost and responsive to changes in market circumstances.

The view expressed in the Readings are, as always in IEA publications, those of the authors, not of the Institute (which has no corporate view), its Trustees, Advisers or Directors. We appreciate the willingness of the commentators to take the debate forward from our original paper; they have produced a stimulating set of views and proposals.

September 2000
JOHN BLUNDELL   *COLIN ROBINSON*
General Director,   *Editorial Director,*
Institute of Economic Affairs   *Institute of Economic Affairs;*
                                                     Professor of Economics,
                                                     University of Surrey

vi

Foreword

MARKETS REQUIRE SUPPORTING INSTITUTIONS. To make the process of transacting as socially productive as possible, people must follow certain rules which constrain and govern their behaviour. They must accept the property rights of others, they must know what it means to come to a 'contract', they must not trespass or otherwise infringe the rights of their neighbours or act 'negligently' towards them. The survival of these market-supporting institutions depends upon the existence of sanctions to punish non-compliance. Markets, in other words, could hardly be said to exist without some form of legal framework to 'regulate' their operation.

At this level of generality the opening proposition is hardly contentious. The disagreements begin when we broach questions about the *source* of the regulatory framework. Where do the rules come from? Who makes them? Who decides on the penalties for non-compliance and who provides the policing? Until fairly recently, economists in the US and UK had considered these issues to be a somewhat peripheral part of their sphere of study. In so far as they were considered, for example in public finance, the prevailing view up to the end of the 1960s (and a view still widely held) was that 'the state' had the task of establishing and enforcing the rules that would enable markets to perform optimally. The provision of a legal and regulatory framework was a kind of 'output' of the state – indeed, 'law and order', fairly widely interpreted, was a classical rationale of the state.[1]

Perhaps the penchant of economists for setting themselves theoretical puzzles led to their somewhat naïve view of the state as a monopoly rule-setter and enforcer. There seemed no logical alternative solution to the 'pure public goods' problem. These goods confer benefits jointly on all citizens. Given the additional

---

[1] One example from the era is W.J. Baumol, *Welfare Economics and the Theory of the State*, London: G. Bell and Sons, 1965.

vii

assumption that it is impossible to exclude people from receiving the benefits of public goods once they are produced, economists deduced that people would always 'free ride' and that only where a state was powerful enough to prevent opportunism and compel compliance could this problem be solved. Regulatory intervention was for a period, therefore, somewhat uncritically recommended wherever 'public good-type problems' arose, and in the absence of any very deep study of institutions and their historical evolution it was possible to believe that they arose all over the place.

Only gradually has it dawned upon economists that the idea of state activity as the only source of regulatory control and enforcement is theoretically flawed and historically contradicted. If there are great social benefits from achieving some objective, solutions to the free-rider problem tend to emerge spontaneously. In other words, the *a priori* assumption of classical public finance that it is impossible (infinitely costly) to exclude non-payers from benefiting from a public good is extremely suspect. Once it becomes merely 'costly' to solve the problem by private means, the relevant issue is to compare these costs with the costs of government action. In other words, solutions to so-called 'market failures' require comparative institutional analysis rather than the introduction of a single remedy – state regulation. Even that most famous of public goods, the lighthouse, discussed in economics textbooks for decades, seems historically to have been provided by private means long before the impossibility of such an eventuality had been formalised.[2]

The recent development of evolutionary and game theoretic ideas in economics also seems to be playing a part in the changing conception of government regulation. Contractors see their own self-interest as best served by honesty rather than cheating if there is a sufficient probability of repeat dealing. The discipline of continuous dealings and the value of a good reputation are more significant in market economies as defences against opportunism than armies of inspectors. Conventions may emerge spontaneously from repeated interactions which are only later codified and

---

[2] See R.H. Coase, 'The Lighthouse in Economics', *Journal of Law and Economics*, Vol.17, No.2, 1974, pp. 357–376.

incorporated into a body of formal law. As has been recognised by legal theorists for many years, institutions which have become inextricably associated with state-enforced law pre-date it: 'Nothing is more silly than to say that the law made private property. The fact is the exact opposite. Private property came to exist and it made the law.'[3]

The New Institutional Economics refers to those institutions which evolve in the light of repeated experience as 'internal institutions' in contrast to rules designed and imposed by political action (external institutions). A significant historical example is the '*lex mercatoria*':

'The medieval Law Merchant was based on certain legal principles, such as equality before the law, which was a path breaking deviation from the feudal class law prevailing at the time. It covered certain customs of trade that were adjudicated by arbitrators who were part of the merchant profession. It was internal law, which was at times formalised but which was enforced without recourse to officials with public power.'[4]

The appropriate division of regulatory responsibility between internal institutions of varying degrees of formality and external government-imposed institutions is of enormous current interest. The issues involved are inherently contentious and difficult to resolve. If the old view of government action as entirely benign seems now to be hopelessly flawed, any contrary assumption that private action is always preferable to state regulation would seem to be equally Panglossian.

In this *IEA Occasional Paper*, John Blundell and Colin Robinson explore the logic of government regulation and the possibilities of alternative voluntary forms of regulation. They use public choice analysis to argue that there is a remorseless tendency for government regulation to be pushed to levels at which marginal social benefits are well below the resulting marginal social costs.

---

[3] John Maxcy Zane, *The Story of Law*, Indianapolis: Liberty Fund Inc., Second Edition, reprinted 1998, p. 147.

[4] Wolfgang Kasper and Manfred E. Streit, *Institutional Economics: Social Order and Public Policy*, Aldershot: Edward Elgar for The Locke Institute, 1998, p. 358.

They show that important areas of economic life are still regulated by voluntary means (Section 11); that these methods do not contain the same in-built tendencies towards over-regulation; and that a more imaginative legal framework might permit this area of 'private' regulation to expand further (Section 12).

All IEA papers contain the views of their authors, not those of the Institute. Although, in this case, the authors are IEA Directors, the IEA has no corporate view and publishes the paper as a stimulating contribution to an important debate on the future of regulation.

July 1999   *MARTIN RICKETTS*
Chairman, IEA Academic Advisory Council;
Professor of Economic Organisation,
University of Buckingham

The Authors

John Blundell was educated at King's School, Macclesfield, and at the London School of Economics. He headed the Press, Research and Parliamentary Liaison Office at the Federation of Small Businesses, 1977–82, and was a Lambeth Borough Councillor, 1978–82. From 1982 to 1993 he lived in the US where he was, *inter alia*, President, Institute for Humane Studies, 1988–91, President, Atlas Economic Research Foundation, 1987–91, President, Congressional Schools of Virginia, 1988–92, President, Charles G. Koch and Claude R. Lambe Charitable Foundation, 1991–92.

He assumed his duties as General Director of the Institute of Economic Affairs on 1 January 1993.

He also served as co-founder and Chairman, 1993–97, of the Institute for Children, Boston, MA; founder director, 1991–93, Institute for Justice, Washington DC; International Trustee, 1988–93, The Fraser Institute, Vancouver, BC; and founder trustee of the Buckeye Institute, Dayton, OH.

He is a director of Fairbridge, a director of the Atlas Economic Research Foundation (UK), Chairman of the Executive Committee of the Board of Atlas Economic Research Foundation (USA), and a Board member of the Institute for Humane Studies at George Mason University, Fairfax, VA, the Institute for Economic Studies (Europe) in Paris, France, and the Mont Pélerin Society.

Colin Robinson was educated at the University of Manchester, and then worked for 11 years as a business economist before being appointed to the chair of Economics at the University of Surrey in 1968.

Professor Robinson has written more than 20 books and monographs and over 150 papers, mainly on energy economics and policy. For the IEA, he has written *A Policy for Fuel?* (IEA Occasional Paper No.31, 1969); *Competition for Fuel* (Supplement to Occasional Paper No.31, 1971); *The Energy 'Crisis' and British Coal* (IEA Hobart Paper No.59, 1974); (with Eileen

Marshall) *What Future for British Coal?* (IEA Hobart Paper No.89, 1981), and *Can Coal Be Saved?* (IEA Hobart Paper No.105, 1985); *Competition in Electricity? The Government's Proposals for Privatising Electricity Supply* (IEA Inquiry No.2, March 1988); *Making a Market in Energy,* IEA Current Controversies No.3, December 1992; *Energy Policy: Errors, Illusions and Market Realities* (IEA Occasional Paper No.90, October 1993). He has contributed chapters to *Privatisation & Competition* (IEA Hobart Paperback No.28, 1989) and to four volumes in the 'Regulating Utilities' series.

Professor Robinson became a member of the IEA's Advisory Council in 1982 and was appointed its Editorial Director in 1992. He was appointed a Trustee of the Wincott Foundation in 1993. He received the British Institute of Energy Economists' award as 'Economist of the Year 1992' and the 'Outstanding Contribution to the Profession' award in 1998 from the International Association for Energy Economics.

Authors of Commentaries

Norman Barry is professor of social and political theory at the University of Buckingham. He has previously taught at the University of Exeter, the Queen's University of Belfast and the University of Central England. His books include *Hayek's Social and Economic Philosophy, An Introduction to Modern Political Theory, Welfare and Business Ethics.* He has contributed to academic journals in political philosophy, welfare theory and the social and moral theory of capitalism. He is a member of the Academic Advisory Councils of the Institute of Economic Affairs (London) and the David Hume Institute (Edinburgh).

David D. Boaz is executive vice president of the Cato Institute, Washington, DC. He is the author of *Libertarianism: A Primer* (1997) and editor of *The Libertarian Reader.* He is a leading authority on domestic issues like educational choice, drug legalization, the growth of government, and the rise of libertarianism and is a frequent guest on national television and radio shows. He is a former editor of *New Guard* magazine and was executive director of the Council for a Competitive Economy prior to joining Cato in 1981.

Christopher Fildes is the financial columnist of *The Daily Telegraph* and *The Spectator*. He is also a director of the The Spectator (1828) Ltd. Educated at Clifton and Balliol College, Oxford, he has worked as a financial journalist, editor and broadcaster since the early 1960s. In 1978 and 1986 he received the Wincott Award, regarded as the senior award for financial journalism. In 1994 he was appointed OBE for services to financial journalism. In 1999 he was awarded the degree of Doctor of Letters (honoris causa) by the University of Sheffield.

Christopher Haskins grew up in Co. Wicklow, Ireland, graduating from Trinity College Dublin in 1959. He joined Northern Foods in 1962 and was appointed Chairman in 1986, becoming its Non-Executive Chairman in 1998. In March 1998 he also became Non-Executive Chairman of the Leicester-based dairy company, Express Dairies plc. He was created a Life Peer in June 1998. He has advised both British and Irish Governments on agricultural, economic and environmental options and currently holds part-time government positions as: Chairman of the Better Regulation Task Force, a member of the New Deal Task Force, and a member of the Board of the Yorkshire and Humber Regional Development Agency ('Yorkshire Forward').

Randall S. Kroszner is Professor of Economics at the University of Chicago's Graduate School of Business and Associate Director of the George J. Stigler Center for the Study of Economy and the State. He is Faculty Research Fellow of the National Bureau of Economic Research and, during 1999–2000, was the John M. Olin Fellow in law and Economics at the University of Chicago Law School. Professor Kroszner has served as an economist on the US President's Council of Economic Advisers and has been a consultant to the IMF, World Bank, US Securities and Exchange Commission, and the US Federal Reserve. He has published extensively in scholarly and policy journals Professor Kroszner received his PhD from Harvard in 1990.

Graeme Leach has been Chief Economist at the Institute of Directors (IoD) since August 1998. The IoD represents 68,000 members worldwide. Prior to joining the IoD he was an Associate Director at the Henley Centre, analysing future economic and social change. He has also worked as economic adviser to the Scottish Provident Investment Group and as a senior economic consultant with Pieda.

Yesmin Yilmaz is completing her PhD. in Economics at George Mason University, Fairfax, VA. Her dissertation investigates alternatives to government regulation in the areas of quality and safety. Yesim holds a BA in Political Science from Bogazici University, Istanbul, Turkey, and an MA in Economics from George Mason University. She currently heads the Business Studies Program for an on-line education company.

Acknowledgements

We thank John Longworth of Tesco for originally challenging us to think the unthinkable about the regulatory state.

We also thank Professor Martin Ricketts of the University of Buckingham, IEA Trustee and Chairman of its Academic Advisory Council. Because the authors are IEA Directors, the normal internal practice of managing a blind review process was not possible. Consequently that process was, in accordance with IEA Board policy, effectively sub-contracted to Professor Ricketts.

We thank the referees he recruited for their helpful comments on an earlier draft. Further useful comments were made by our colleague Gerald Frost. None of the above is responsible for the conclusions of the paper, nor for any errors which may remain.

May 1999   J. B.
                                                                                            C. R.

Regulation Without the State
JOHN BLUNDELL and COLIN ROBINSON

1. Government versus Voluntary Regulation

'REGULATION' IS NOW A COMMON TOPIC OF CON-VERSATION. Businessmen discuss it constantly because it has such an impact on their activities; pressure groups lobby for it; TV news programmes run segments on it; and private individuals talk about the intimate effects it has on their lives. Nearly all media debates on current issues end up with suggestions for new regulations. Generally, the term 'regulation' is used as shorthand to mean attempts by governments, driven by a myriad of reasons, to make rules for others, whether by legislation or by administrative action.

Rules are an essential part of life. But making them is not necessarily a government function: they can be (and usually are) established through voluntary action. The institutional arrange-ments which govern the conduct of both individuals and organisations have, in mature liberal democracies such as those in Western Europe and North America, evolved over many centuries in the light of experience.[1] It would not be possible to live relatively orderly lives, as we do, unless over the years rules for living and standards of behaviour had emerged and developed into social norms (some integrated, *ex post*, into a framework of law and order).

Contrary to conventional wisdom, the alternative to state regu-lation is not a regulatory void, but a range of voluntary arrange-ments. In practice, both types of regulation are to be found in Britain and other democratic societies although, in the clamour

---

[1] Douglass C. North, *Understanding the Process of Economic Change*, Occasional Paper 106, London: Institute of Economic Affairs, March 1999.

1

for instant solutions which often follows a perceived 'crisis', state regulation may crowd out voluntary solutions because of the widespread assumption, fostered by politicians with short time-horizons, that government always has a remedy which will bring more benefits than costs.[2] Experience suggests this assumption is not well founded. Much government regulation has unintended consequences: as one regulation fails to achieve its intended goals, another follows in the hope that it will succeed. Thus, the regulatory state leads to the accumulation of layers of regulation, one effect of which is to reduce democratic accountability.[3]

This brief paper examines how government regulation arises; considers the costs of regulation, their incidence and the problems which emerge; describes some examples of voluntary regulation; and concludes with some recommendations for increasing the scope of these voluntary means. Its intention is to promote discussion of the respective scale and scope of government and voluntary regulation.

2. Some Problems of Principle

REGULATION BY GOVERNMENT CAN TAKE a variety of forms, ranging from the extreme of central planning of economic activity, to forms of planning without coercion ('indicative planning'), to market-improving measures intended to make the outcome more like that of the neo-classical economist's ideal of 'perfect competition'. Economic planning in all its varieties has been exposed to the most damaging criticisms of principle, and is widely regarded as discredited in practice because of the experiences of the Soviet and other planned economies.

But, even though the idea of market improvement is vulnerable to the same criticisms as those levelled at economic planning, the idea survives. Indeed, it remains influential in providing the

---

[2] One of the IEA's earliest papers argued against government regulation of hire purchase agreements other than through general monetary and fiscal policy: Ralph Harris, Arthur Seldon and Margot Naylor, *Hire Purchase in a Free Society*, IEA, 1958, Second Edition 1959, Third Edition 1961.

[3] Norman Barry, 'The Market, Liberty and the Regulatory State', *Economic Affairs*, Vol. 14, No.4, June 1994, pp. 5–11, and John O'Sullivan, *Conservatism, Democracy and National Identity*, London: Centre for Policy Studies, 1999.

intellectual justification for government action, *inter alia*, to promote health and safety, to safeguard the natural environment, to subsidise education, to enhance job security, to set minimum wages, to avoid worker 'exploitation', and to protect investors from the choices they make.

In reality, the establishment and growth of regulation may have little connection with such ideas. Much of it is evidently the outcome of 'rent-seeking' behaviour by pressure groups and regulators (see Sections 4 to 7 below) which see advantages in the introduction and expansion of government regulation. But the intellectual underpinnings of the case for regulation are important because they provide a cloak of respectability for a process which is often far from worthy.

The intellectual case, as used by mainstream economists, generally justifies government regulation on the ground that a particular market can be improved because it 'fails' – that is, it does not achieve 'public interest' objectives. Thus, it is claimed, the state should step in to improve on what would otherwise be the market outcome. But there is a fundamental problem with this 'market failure' approach to policy-making: it takes as its standard of what is desirable the mainstream economist's model of the long-run equilibrium of perfect competition.[4] Since that is an idealised state which can never be found in practice, measuring real-world markets against such a standard means that every market appears to 'fail'. Consequently, use of the market-failure model leads inexorably to recommendations for widespread government intervention across the economy – not necessarily because there are genuine problems with markets but because performance does not measure up to an unattainable ideal. Many 'failures' are, in reality, part of normal market processes rather than departures from a state which, in practice, could be emulated.[5]

Moreover, the market-failure approach implies perfect government – an altruistic and omniscient body which can detect and

---

[4] Mark Blaug, 'Classical Economics', in Eatwell, Milgate and Newman (eds.), *The New Palgrave – A Dictionary of Economics*, Vol. 1, London: Macmillan, 1987.

[5] Israel M. Kirzner, *How Markets Work: Disequilibrium, Entrepreneurship and Discovery,* Hobart Paper No.133, London: Institute of Economic Affairs, 1997.

will unswervingly pursue the 'public interest'.[6] This benevolent government is assumed to detect failures in markets and then correct them, without regard to the self-interest of its members or more general political considerations. The comparison of 'imperfect' markets with perfect governments is obviously loaded and leads to demands for more government action than would be made if the imperfections of government were taken into account. When responding to the assertion that government intervention was required to solve a particular problem, Alfred Marshall is said to have replied: 'Do you mean government, all wise, all just, all powerful, or government as it now is?'[7]

Curiously, many people who press for more government regulation appear unaware that, underlying their arguments, is a model of how markets and governments work to which they would almost certainly not subscribe. Furthermore, given the faults in the underlying regulatory model, practical problems in implemention are inevitable. Some of these problems are outlined below, beginning with the costs of regulation.

3. A Question of Costs

MOST PEOPLE WOULD AGREE that the reasons governments usually give for imposing regulations are worthy. People wish, *inter alia*, to be healthy and safe, to minimise adverse effects on the environment of human activity, to have their children well-educated, to ensure workers are properly treated, and to avoid rogue selling in financial markets. The question then is whether these desirable aims to which most – if not all – subscribe are better attained primarily by government regulation or primarily by voluntary action.

As government regulation has grown in recent years, serious concerns have emerged in European countries, the United States and Japan about its costs even though they are difficult to estimate. Government budgetary costs are known but are only a small part

---

[6] The 'public choice' approach, which criticises the perfect government assumption, is explained in Gordon Tullock, *The Vote Motive*, Hobart Paperback No.9, Institute of Economic Affairs, Second Impression, 1978. See also William C. Mitchell, *Government as It Is,* Hobart Paper No.109, IEA, 1988.

[7] A. E. Benians, *Memorials of Alfred Marshall*, London: Macmillan, 1926.

of the total; the much larger costs of complying with regulations ('compliance costs') which fall on organisations and individuals, can be estimated, but the 'invisible' costs (broadly, adverse effects on enterprise and technological development, as explained in 8 below) are largely unknown.

Estimates have been made of the costs of federal regulation in the United States, including compliance costs but not invisible costs. One study puts compliance costs at about $700 billion, dwarfing the costs borne by federal government agencies of some $15 billion. These estimated compliance costs represent about 9 per cent of United States GDP or almost $7,000 per family (about 19 per cent of average two-earner family income).[8] The main trends in the US are for the costs of 'economic' regulation to decrease because of deregulation in some major industries (natural gas, telecommunications, airlines and most recently electricity), while the costs of 'social' (including environmental) regulation have increased sharply, doubling in real terms in the last 10 years.

Regulatory costs are not so well documented in other countries. But there is no reason to believe that the huge disparity between the regulatory costs borne by government and total regulatory costs is unique to the United States: as explained in 4 below, the disparity is inherent in the process of government regulation. Moreover, observation suggests it is not only in the United States where the growth of government 'social' regulation proceeds apace. In other developed countries, despite reductions in trade barriers and deregulation of the utilities and some transport sectors, this form of regulation appears to have increased.

4. Who Bears the Costs of Regulation?

THE DISPARITY BETWEEN TOTAL COSTS and costs which fall on regulators is highly significant. Costs borne by government are only about 2 per cent of compliance costs in the United States

---

[8] Thomas D. Hopkins, *Regulatory Costs in Profile*, Center for the Study of American Business, Policy Study No.132, Rochester, New York, August 1996. The Center estimates that in 1999 federal regulation spending will be almost $18 billion: see *Investors Business Daily*, 24 February 1999. For a study which surveys US regulatory costs and different ways of measuring them (for example, by counting pages of regulations), see Clyde Wayne Crews, Jr., *Ten Thousand Commandments: A Policymaker's Snapshot of the Federal Regulatory State*, 1998 edition, Washington DC: Competitive Enterprise Institute, January 1998.

and would be a smaller percentage still of the total costs of regulation if invisible costs could be included. Thus, as far as government and government regulatory bodies are concerned, the bulk of the costs of regulation are 'external' (that is, they fall on others); this, more than any other factor, seems to explain the impetus behind the growth of regulation.

Indeed, the arguments used by mainstream economists for introducing regulation can be stood rather neatly on their head. The mainstream case is that there are 'externalities' which private markets will not take into account: thus government should intervene to ensure any external costs and benefits are taken into account. But, in practice, the introduction of regulation creates new externalities. Costs which would have been 'internal' (and therefore taken into account by decision-makers) are not borne by regulators and, therefore, no matter how well-meaning they may be, these costs become externalities as far as they are concerned. In such circumstances, with the bulk of the costs of regulation not falling on those who regulate, the amount of regulation is likely to be expanded far beyond its 'efficient' level – which would occur when it had extended just to the point at which the costs of another regulation would exceed its benefits. In short, though market failure is the common reason for urging government regulation, the institution of regulation itself leads to a different form of failure.

5. Over-Regulation

THE PROCESSES OUTLINED ABOVE SUGGEST that government regulation will always and everywhere exceed the level which could be justified if all its costs and benefits were taken into account. Thus, 'over-regulation' is to be expected.

Over-regulation is now a common complaint in many countries, as has been acknowledged by the OECD whose Public Management Service has proposed an OECD-wide study of alternatives to regulation.[9] Deregulatory initiatives have started in several countries, including the United States, Japan and Britain. In Britain,

---

[9] *Focus*, Public Management Gazette, No.8, Paris: Organisation for Economic Co-operation and Development, March 1998, p. 1. See also a comment on the US Regulatory Improvement Act 1997 in National Center for Policy Analysis, *Brief Analysis* 258, 2 March 1998.

6

a McKinsey study in 1998 claimed that '... regulations imposed to achieve socially desirable outcomes often had the unintended impact of damaging employment and growth'.[10] Similarly, the chairman of Britain's Better Regulation Task Force, Christopher (now Lord) Haskins, has argued that Britain has too much regulation and that private alternatives can '... deliver objectives more effectively and at less cost'. As he puts it:

'The voluntary action of individuals or groups of individuals can also achieve objectives much more efficiently and effectively than the state. Too many people have come to depend on the government to provide protection they could perfectly well organise themselves.'[11]

Government regulation is difficult to change because of the lengthy and often complex political process involved. By the time a regulation is enacted, it often relates to a world that no longer exists (see below). Moreover, regulations often outlive the circumstances which brought them into being: Britain's Sunday Trading regulations are a classic example of regulations which could not keep pace with the times.[12] Attitudes towards regulation might be more sceptical if greater attention was focused on its past record, and upon the relative experience of countries which reacted to particular problems without state regulation. A recent study on the regulatory and other constraints on big business by two British sociologists concludes:

'... our institutions are quite unresponsive because we live in an unreflexive society. We are always peering forward at tomorrow's possible dangers and yet it is only by considering the ways in which we foolishly over-reacted to illusory techno-moral panics in the past that we can know how to react to them rationally. ... We must look backwards, and respond with scepticism.'[13]

---

[10] 'Regulatory Barriers can damage employment and growth', report of a seminar on the McKinsey findings, *The Financial Times*, 15 May 1998. The McKinsey report was subsequently published as McKinsey Global Institute, *Driving Productivity and Growth in the UK Economy*, London: McKinsey, 1998.

[11] Christopher Haskins, 'Rules and More Rules', *The Financial Times*, 13 May 1998.

[12] John Burton, *Whither Sunday Trading? The Case for Deregulation*, Hobart Paper No.123, London: Institute of Economic Affairs, 1993.

[13] Mark Neil and Christie Davis, *The Corporation Under Siege*, London: Social Affairs Unit, 1998, p. 103.

Anxieties about excessive regulatory systems have been enhanced by concern that very detailed ('prescriptive') regulation may not be compatible with the need for companies to remain nimble and competitive in markets which are changing rapidly under the impact of 'globalisation'. In the words of Murray Weidenbaum, former Chairman of the US President's Council of Economic Advisers:

'In no nation is there a government agency with a mission to depress the economy or to accelerate inflation. However, many government actions – especially taxation, government spending and regulation – have those undesirable effects. Regulatory costs are especially insidious. They are a hidden tax severely reducing the competitiveness of domestic businesses at a time when they face an increasingly global marketplace.' [14]

In Britain's case, the total volume of regulation is growing as a result of its membership of the European Union. Comprehensive data about EU regulation is in short supply. Nevertheless, it would seem that despite Jacques Santer's promise that the introduction of the subsidiarity principle would mean 'fewer and better' rules, the volume of EU regulation is continuing to expand. According to data based on EU figures, the total number of EC/EU legal acts in force rose from 1,947 in 1973, to 14,729 in 1990 and to 23,027 by 1996.[15] A further indication of just how active is the Brussels regulatory machine is that the number of pages produced by the EU Publication Office more than doubled during a seven-year period – from 886,996 in 1989 to 1,916,808 in 1996. Compliance costs will inevitably be higher in those states where national interpretations of EU rules have been more stringent than the original rulings themselves, as has often been the case in Britain.[16] And they will also be higher in those countries where there is a

[14] Murray Weidenbaum, *Recasting The Role of Government to Promote Economic Prosperity*, Pfizer Forum, *The Financial Times*, 12 May 1998.

[15] Jens-Peter Bonde, MEP, 'Centralisation will Continue', *Eurofacts*, 19 December 1997.

[16] Richard North, *Death by Regulation: The Butchery of the British Meat Industry*, IEA Health and Welfare Unit Health Series No.12, May 1993.

strong tradition of obeying the law than in those in which respect for legal authority is weak.

6. Interest Groups and Regulation

ANOTHER REASON WHY REGULATION IS ESTABLISHED and tends to grow is that interest groups of all kinds can benefit significantly from regulation. The 'rent-seeking' process by which pressure groups bend government policies in their own favour explains the commonly-observed fact that government policies often appear to be dominated by the interests of producers and other organised groups rather than by 'the public interest'.

The underlying reason why organised groups are so influential in regulation (and other government policy-making) is that the potential benefits of regulation are concentrated on their members whereas the costs of regulation are dispersed over large numbers of consumers or even the whole population. Take, as an example, an industry which could gain if the government established a regulation which gave its members protection from imports. If the industry is successful, all the benefits (for example, increased employment in the short term in that industry and higher wages) will accrue to its members. The costs (for example, higher prices for the products concerned) will fall on large numbers of consumers.

Because benefits are concentrated, the industry has a powerful incentive to invest resources in lobbying for protection – for instance, producing information about job losses and other problems which it will claim will arise if government does not act in accordance with its wishes. Because it will be better informed about conditions in the industry than government, it will expect to have a good chance of success.

Individual consumers, on the other hand, will each face only small costs if the regulation is introduced. Consequently, they have little incentive to invest in the time and other costs which they would incur if they opposed the regulation. Many consumers may well not realise that there are costs involved. Hence, though there may be millions of 'invisible victims' of a regulation and the total costs may be far in excess of the benefits to the organised group, the victims may in practice mount only feeble opposition or not oppose the regulation at all.

9

Agriculture, in particular, is riddled with examples of rent-seeking, concentrated benefits and dispersed costs. In *Beyond Good Intentions*,[17] Doug Bandow tells the story of US honey manufacturers. About 2,500 of them exist and they receive an annual subsidy from the US Agriculture Department of $100 million ($40,000 each on average). In 1987, a tiny change in the regulations governing these subsidies led to the 15 largest producers garnering an extra $6 million a year or $400,000 each on average. While for each producer, there was a huge gain, the average loss to each US citizen was extremely small – about 2 cents, or much less than the cost of a stamp to send a letter of complaint.

It is because the benefits of regulation are concentrated but the costs are dispersed that the beneficiaries of regulation exert more lobbying power than the victims and have an undue weight in policy-making.

7. Problems Inherent in Regulated Markets

BECAUSE LOBBY GROUPS OFTEN FIND IT in their interests to press for regulation (as explained above), and because regulators do not bear the costs of much of their activity, a number of consequences for regulated markets emerge. Some of them are explained below.

Regulatory Bodies Tend to Expand

The desire to build empires is a common feature of all organisations but the ability to do so, in competitive markets, is constrained by the actions of rivals. However, there is no straightforward way of assessing objectively how much regulation would be beneficial. Thus it is difficult to keep a check on the actions of regulatory bodies and regulatory growth is driven by the discrepancy between the costs borne by regulators and the total costs of regulatory action (3 and 4 above). Because others shoulder most of the costs, regulatory bodies have no incentive to minimise costs: instead they are likely to favour standards which stretch the limits of known technology.[18] In health

---

[17] Douglas Bandow, *Beyond Good Intentions*, Westchester, Illinois: Crossway, 1988.

[18] As explained in 8 below, regulation is likely to hinder technological progress. Thus, though regulators may aim for the limits, the technology will probably be less advanced in a regulated industry than if regulation was absent.

and safety matters, for example, they will want to show they have done everything technically possible in order to avoid blame if accidents occur. Insisting on cost-benefit analyses of proposed regulatory action is of little value because all the relevant costs and benefits lie in the future: thus they are uncertain and can only be assessed subjectively. The self-interest of regulators will, in general, make them tend to exaggerate benefits, under-estimate costs and over-estimate the demand for action on their part.[19]

Some Firms Seek Regulation and Competition Is Suppressed

Established firms in an industry may welcome regulation as a means of keeping out potential entrants (by raising the costs of entry). Research in the United States has established that in the late 19th century regulation was often sought by the incumbents.[20] Other research suggests that the 1938 US federal minimum wage law was actually an attempt by Massachusetts politicians and textile workers to hamper competition from textiles produced by low-wage labour in the Southern states.[21] More recently, it has been clear in Britain that large organisations have, in general, been less resistant to impositions such as a minimum wage than smaller ones. The consequence is that a regulated market is often one in which competition has been suppressed and consumers therefore suffer from higher prices and poorer service standards than would otherwise exist.

Firms May Capture Regulators

Once regulation is in place, the regulator must rely to a large extent on information provided by incumbents (that is, there is 'information asymmetry') and so there is some dependence on the regulated company. Furthermore, the regulator may see his or her career prospects in the regulated industry; there is a history of

---

[19] For a critique of efforts to assess the costs and benefits of regulation in the United States, see Robert W. Hahn, 'Policy Watch: Analysis of the Benefits and Costs of Regulation', *Journal of Economic Perspectives*, Vol. 12, No. 4, Fall 1998.

[20] George J. Stigler, 'The Theory of Economic Regulation', *Bell Journal of Economics and Management,* Spring 1971.

[21] B. W. Folsom Jr., 'The Minimum Wage's Disreputable Origins', *The Wall Street Journal,* 27 May 1998.

11

regulators subsequently finding work in industries for which they formerly exercised responsibility. 'Regulatory capture' may therefore occur as the regulator becomes sympathetic to producers and may act in their interests. Or the regulator might be captured by some other pressure group (such as 'environmentalists'). Thus, consumers may suffer from regulation, if regulators act in the interests of producers or other groups. Numerous studies have noted this tendency within the US system of regulation,[22] though it is probably less prevalent in Britain (see 9 below).

Regulation Is Popular with Politicians

The popularity of regulation is partly because it appears to be a direct attempt to 'do something' about a problem. The news media, often urged on by pressure groups, seize on accidents, apparent emergencies, and examples of human error of all kinds. They demand action, invoking the 'precautionary principle', even though there is often considerable scientific uncertainty about the relevant issues and the necessary action. A recent example is the draconian action taken in Britain to combat the supposed risk of BSE ('mad cow disease') being connected with Creutzfeldt-Jakob disease in humans. More generally, the political response to such events is likely to be an inquiry, new regulations and perhaps even a new regulatory body. The government may be well aware that such a 'knee-jerk' reaction will lead to little, if any, public benefit: it is done to assuage the demands for action caused by asymmetries in news reporting (the dominance of bad news).

8. High Costs and Perverse Consequences

REGULATION THUS ACQUIRES ITS OWN MOMENTUM which has little to do with considerations of the public interest. It is popular with powerful pressure groups, with regulators and with politicians: because its costs are dispersed, consumers who lose from regulation lack the incentive to oppose it.

Yet the total costs of regulation are substantial. As explained above, some of them (such as government budgetary costs and the compliance costs of those affected by regulations) can be

---

[22] Stigler, *op.cit.*, and Sam Peltzman, 'Toward a More General Theory of Regulation', *Journal of Law and Economics,* August 1976.

estimated. But the invisible costs are likely to be much greater. They consist of the higher prices and lower standards for consumers which are mentioned above; the general tendency for producer interests to be favoured by regulation; and, perhaps most important of all, the dampening effect on entrepreneurship, innovation and subsequent technological and managerial development. Rigid rules which inevitably fail to take into account future developments in technology make product, marketing and other innovations difficult: consequently, current practice is frozen and people's lives improve less than they would otherwise have done.

Regulation by the state can be very crude in its approach to setting rules. For whatever reason, attention focuses on a particular process or situation. A regulation based on today's knowledge and technology is passed. Even though bureaucrats (for reasons discussed in 7 above) press for high standards, before long knowledge expands, technology changes and better ways (previously unknown) of doing things emerge. However, the introduction of these prospective innovations is hampered by the regulation which was meant to help matters. Until the bureaucrats or politicians return to the issue, the regulation will not reflect such changes in know-how. On the other hand, market-driven regulation will tend to change in small increments as knowledge, technology and other relevant variables change.

Government regulation therefore rests on uncertain foundations of principle and leads to practical difficulties. It is not legitimate simply to *assume*, as advocates of government action frequently do, that it will on balance be beneficial and achieve that elusive concept, the 'public interest'.[23] Not only are the costs of regulation likely to be high, it will almost invariably crowd out market solutions to the problems with which regulation is intended to deal. Over time, a growing edifice of regulation, brought about by empire-building and the other tendencies mentioned above, may well hinder progress in meeting people's wants, including their demands for health, safety, environmental protection and other aspects of life. The most notable cases of failures to accede to consumer demands appear to be in areas where choice is restricted

---

[23] See, for example, J. High (ed.), *Regulation: Economic Theory and History*, University of Michigan Press, 1991, for critiques of the 'public interest' theory.

by state action – such as education and transport and, before privatisation, in the British nationalised industries – so that monopoly prevails and suppliers, in the absence of competitors, are careless about their reputations.

Furthermore, state regulation has often had perverse results. In recent memory Britain has been subject to housing controls that dried up the supply of rented accommodation, wage restrictions that resulted in a mismatch of skills and employment opportunities, and price controls that served to increase the inflationary pressures they were meant to reduce. In one of the areas in which its use is most often recommended – environmental protection – state regulation has not merely achieved perverse side-effects, but done so on a remarkable scale. The former Soviet Union and the countries of central and eastern Europe are obvious examples of the disastrous effects on the environment of an extreme form of regulation (central planning). But the nationalised electricity supply industry in England and Wales, which was forced by governments to rely on coal and nuclear power, offers another example of an excessively polluting activity brought about by government action (and also of how government action can reduce security of supply).[24]

Even where the consequences of regulation are not so widespread and serious as those just cited, the exercise of human ingenuity often results in unintended effects. For example, a recent article sets out some of the effects of a US regulation in the 1970s which required that children's pyjamas be flame-resistant.[25] The regulation effectively ruled out the use of cotton but, because parents wanted (more comfortable) cotton sleepwear for their children, manufacturers gave it labels such as 'brushed cotton sets' rather than pyjamas. Cotton sleepwear was allowed in 1996 when it was realised the old regulation was not working. However, the new regulation said it must be tight-fitting (to specific measurements) to avoid the risk of burns: it is easily evaded by parents who buy larger sizes to compensate for the tighter fit. There is

[24] Colin Robinson, *Energy Policy: Errors, Illusions and Market Realities*, Occasional Paper No.90, London: Institute of Economic Affairs, 1993.

[25] Jacob Sullum, 'Compromising Kids' Safety for Comfort', *Conservative Chronicle*, 17 June 1998.

considerable waste of resources in this kind of game in which regulators set rules, those who are regulated avoid the rules, regulators try again, there is more evasion, and so on.

9. Regulation Without the State

THOUGH MARKETS ARE POPULARLY BELIEVED TO 'FAIL', in practice the principal way in which the objectives of regulation are achieved is through the everyday interaction of consumers and producers. There is a demand from individuals, whether in their consumer or their producer roles, for health and safety, worker protection, safeguards for the environment and other such desirable features of life. As living standards increase and consumers' more basic wants are satisfied, demand for those features appears to increase at a faster rate than income. This effect can be seen over time in a given country, or by examining a cross-section of countries with different living standards at a particular point in time. It is therefore in the interests of actual and potential suppliers to meet such demands. It is a way to build reputations and to achieve success.

Broadly, voluntary alternatives to state regulation allow markets to work, ensuring that there are legal or other remedies for those who may suffer from the actions of others, and permit market-based forms of protection, such as insurance, voluntary enforcement of standards and perhaps voluntary standard-setting, to flourish. The results are 'imperfect', but so are all conceivable outcomes.

In the absence of any government regulation, the features of life which regulation seeks to supply would be provided, to the extent that they were sought by consumers. Consumers buy bundles of goods and characteristics, not just goods *per se.* Consequently, organisations would compete to protect and enhance their reputations by producing goods with attributes demanded by consumers (including safety in consumption, healthy properties and benign environmental features). A company's reputation is potentially its most important asset: in competitive conditions, companies have strong incentives to strive to enhance their reputations by meeting customer needs and distinguishing their products from those of others, for example by branding.[26] Companies would also compete

---

[26] Daniel B. Klein, *Reputation: Studies in the Voluntary Elicitation of Good Conduct,* University of Michigan Press, 1997.

15

to provide good pay and conditions for their workforces, because they would want to safeguard their reputations in order to obtain and keep the best workers.

Where appropriate, companies would band together to set standards for products and to establish certification procedures in order to give consumers confidence in their purchases. There would be market opportunities to provide independent standard-setting, testing and certification services and so suppliers of such services would appear. Other organisations would provide information services for consumers. The growth of the Internet has led to predictions of greatly enhanced opportunities for consumers through new 'infomediaries',[27] which will help consumers reduce the transactions costs of searching for goods in a complex environment.

Under such a régime, there would probably be much greater use of private insurance than there is now. People would, for instance, protect themselves by insuring against eventualities such as unemployment, sickness and old age, and they would also protect against defects in the goods and services they purchased. Such protections are already built into many mortgage and hire purchase agreements and some credit card purchases.

10. Changing the Incentives of Regulators

ONE WAY TO REDUCE THE QUANTITY OF REGULATION and to limit its adverse effects which would involve relatively little disturbance to the existing régime, is to change the incentives of regulators to make them less prone to empire-building and more inclined to resist the expansion of regulation sought by other interested parties. In this respect, some success has been achieved in British utility regulation by giving regulators a duty to promote or facilitate competition.[28] At the time these duties were imposed, their significance was not fully appreciated, though it was realised that transforming an industry from monopoly to competition required some such provision. However, the duties have had more

---

[27] John Hagel and Marc Singer, *Net Worth: Shaping Markets When Customers Make The Rules,* Boston: Harvard Business School Press, 1999, Ch. 1, and *The McKinsey Quarterly,* No.1, 1999, pp. 7–15.

[28] The wording of the duty differs from regulator to regulator. The weakest duty – to 'facilitate' competition – is in water and sewerage.

pervasive effects than foreseen. Not only have they allowed regulators to take the initiative in promoting entry to markets, they have altered incentives. Regulators know that one of the principal ways in which their actions will be judged (for example, when reappointment is being considered) is the extent to which competition has been promoted in the market they supervise. Consequently, if one accepts that competition is the prime means of safeguarding the interests of consumers by providing them with choice,[29] it follows that British utility regulators will tend to act primarily in the interests of consumers. 'Capture' by producers has certainly not been the serious issue in British utilities that it has been in the United States.

Moreover, the emphasis on competition-promotion means that as competition increases in utility markets, the need for regulation declines. The logical outcome is that eventually regulation covers only genuine 'natural monopoly' areas (such as networks of wires, pipes and tracks).[30] In other words, there is a mechanism within the British utility regulation régime which places a constraint on regulation and should cause regulatory offices to shrink over time.

There are special features of the utilities, such as the market power of the incumbents immediately after privatisation, which made pro-competition duties essential. Nevertheless, the idea of a duty which impels regulators to act in the consumer interest and makes it unattractive to them to expand their empires is capable of much wider application in many markets, not only in Britain, which are now regulated. As one example, a duty to promote competition could be included in the responsibilities of financial regulators to avoid their becoming excessively prescriptive and expansion-prone (as they may become, for example, under the new centralised system in Britain). It would help to avoid the general tightening of regulation and the addition of detail which tend to occur in unconstrained regulatory systems and which severely

---

[29] As the present government does. See, for example, Department for Trade and Industry, *A Fair Deal for Consumers: Modernising The Framework for Utility Regulation – The Response to Consultation*, July 1998, para. 42.

[30] The gas and electricity regulators have already shrunk what were previously believed to be 'natural monopoly' activities by introducing competition into areas such as storage, meter reading and meter provision which were previously monopolised.

hamper market processes. Similar duties could be applied in other regulated areas.

11. Voluntary Forms of Regulation

IT IS USEFUL TO EXAMINE SOME CASES where regulation has emerged naturally, rather than being imposed by governments, to determine if these cases could have wider application.

Standard-Setting and Compliance Procedures

An important distinction must be drawn between the setting of standards and the monitoring and compliance procedures (for example, inspection, testing and certification) which are used to ensure that standards are met. There is considerable experience of the involvement of independent third parties in compliance procedures and some of their involvement in standard setting. In the absence of government regulation both procedures can come into being through voluntary action, as the following examples demonstrate.

The Case of Underwriters Laboratories

In the United States, Underwriters Laboratories (UL) is a private not-for-profit organisation which provides voluntary safety certification for, *inter alia*, electrical appliances, automotive products, medical appliances, alarm systems and chemicals.[31] It not only tests and certifies but also develops standards after a careful and open review process. Although it has rivals it has, over the last 100 years, built up a position as the largest organisation in its field. Such is its reputation, retailers are reluctant to sell goods unless they have certification from UL or one of its competitors, though there is no legal requirement for such certification. Although certification relates only to safety, failure to obtain a certificate would make a product extremely difficult to market. The

---

[31] Further details about Underwriters Laboratories can be found in Yesim Yilmaz, *Private Regulation: A real alternative for regulatory reform*, Policy Analysis No.303, Washington DC: Cato Institute, 20 April 1998, especially pp. 14–16.

voluntary system works well because the standards are well-recognised; manufacturers and retailers therefore have a powerful incentive to comply with them.

As far as efficiency and market responsiveness are concerned, UL is in a fundamentally different position from a government agency. It operates in a competitive market (it has 12 competitors and entry to the market is possible) and so has incentives to keep down its costs and to adapt to changing market circumstances. Moreover, all the costs of standard setting and compliance have to be within the range acceptable to its customers. Consequently, it avoids the bias towards excessive regulation which is likely when the regulatory body bears only a small fraction of the costs of its own activities.

The success of UL – and of the British Standards Institution's 'Kite Mark' scheme – demonstrates the advantages of voluntary action over prescriptive government regulation. The self-interest of companies leads them to seek certification by the regulator and the regulatory body has better incentives than a state regulator.

Green Seal, Scientific Certification Systems, and Eco-Rating

Another example concerns three US agencies which rate products according to how benign they are in environmental terms.[32] Green Seal is a non-profit labelling organisation which aims to help consumers select products that meet specified environmental standards. Like UL, it carries out an extensive review process before setting standards. Products which comply with the standards are awarded the Green Seal of Certification and carry labels which inform consumers about the product's environmental characteristics. The companies concerned sign contracts with Green Seal and compliance is monitored by inspections.

In the same field is Eco-Rating International Inc., a for-profit company which rates products for environmental soundness, using performance scales similar to those employed by financial indices. Scientific Certification Systems also certifies products for environmental characteristics, considering, for example, carbon dioxide and sulphur emissions.

---

[32] *Ibid.*, pp. 20–22.

Consumer Information and Rating Agencies

A natural market response to the demand by consumers for information about products and services is the emergence of organisations which assess the performance, safety and other relevant attributes of products. Companies will perceive the scope for such services and thus will have a market incentive to supply them. Once established, these services will be sought by suppliers which see approval as an important means of enhancing reputation.

In Britain the Consumers' Association (publishers of *Which?*) has emerged, in response to market demand, as an agency which provides information on products and services and rates them for consumers. There are several in the United States,[33] such as the Consumers' Union which evaluates products and publishes the results in its monthly *Consumer Reports*, an annual *Buying Guide*, TV and radio reports, and newspaper articles. *Consumer Reports* has 5 million subscribers. The Good Housekeeping Institute is a product evaluation laboratory which awards the Seal of Good Housekeeping – which includes a warranty that Good Housekeeping will replace a defective product or refund the price within a year of purchase. There is also a Council of Better Business in the United States and Canada which sets high standards for members, provides reports for consumers and also acts as an arbitration body in disputes between its members and consumers. Another example of an arbitration scheme is the one for holiday packages which is offered by British travel agents.

Engineering Insurance

British examples of private certification can be found in safety regulation in some industries – for example, those producing lifts and hoists, steam boilers and transportable gas containers, all potentially dangerous activities. Present legislation requires inspection of the relevant activity by a 'competent person' who provides the necessary safety certification. This function has come naturally to be undertaken by the companies which insure those facilities.

---

[33] *Ibid.*, pp. 28–30.

'Engineering insurance' schemes go back to the middle of the 19th century when there was serious concern about the number of explosions occurring in steam boilers. In order to deal with the problem, companies concerned voluntarily banded together. The system of insurance and inspection that eventually emerged from their efforts evolved to become a flourishing business in its own right. In other words, a market-based solution evolved to meet a need, though it was subsequently backed up by a government requirement for inspection.

Because the engineering insurance companies are subject to normal market incentives, they have adapted to changing circumstances in a way which government regulatory bodies find extremely difficult. As a result the business has developed considerably since its early beginnings when it specialised in steam boilers. Today, Royal and Sun Alliance Engineering's brochure (see Box 1) states that it will provide inspection services (with or without insurance) and technical consultancy services for a wide range of plant and owners. It will cover engineering risks (including business interruptions), construction and transportation risks, and 'electronic' risks (including the financial consequences of computer system breakdowns). Although it provides inspection without insurance, it will not, of course, provide insurance without inspection.

For insurance to be a practicable option, it must be possible to avoid the problems which arise because of hidden information, the two most important of which are those described by economists as 'adverse selection' (those seeking insurance may hide information about themselves) and 'moral hazard' (once insured, companies and individuals may conceal their lack of effort to avoid the relevant risks). In brief, insurance companies have to be able to assess *ex ante* what risks they are running and to monitor *ex post* whether those they have insured are 'shirking'.

Linking inspection to insurance, as in the engineering case, deals neatly with both these problems. Companies need to have clearance by a competent inspector and they also seek insurance in the knowledge that occasionally something will go wrong. The company appreciates that it will obtain insurance only if its facilities are deemed satisfactory after inspection by insurers with long experience in assessing risks in the industries concerned. From the insurer's point of view, its accumulated expertise allows

Box 1

The Birth and Development of Engineering Insurance Companies

As Britain's industrial revolution gathered pace in the 19th century, demand for steam power grew dramatically. Steam boilers were constructed for textile mills and heavy industry, and by 1850 the Midlands and North of England had the highest concentration of steam boilers in the world.

But the design and construction of boilers were at an early stage of technical development, and dangers associated with boilers and the limitations of technical ability were not fully understood. Explosions were frequent as boilers were used at too high pressures. Severe damage to property and substantial loss of lives made these explosions a cause for national concern.

In 1854 a particularly violent explosion, in which 10 people were killed, occurred in Rochdale. As a result of this Sir William Fairbairn, designer of the Lancashire boiler, started gathering scientific and industrial advice and evidence from people who had attended inquests on boiler explosions. His investigations prompted a meeting of engineers, scientists, manufacturers and mill-owners the same year, which led to the formation of the *Association for the Prevention of Steam Boiler Explosions*. This group organised voluntary inspections without responsibility, but was quite ineffective.

In an attempt to develop a more effective solution to boiler explosions, the *Steam Boiler Assurance Company* was formed by merchants and industrialists in 1858. This was the first company both to inspect and insure new and in-service boilers. The company went through a period of rapid expansion, and was reconstructed as the *Boiler Insurance and Steam Power Company* in 1865, a year which also saw the formation of the *National Boiler and General Insurance Company*. This new part of the insurance industry resulted in examinations of engines, mechanical and electrical plants, process machinery, cranes and lifts, coupled with suitable insurance cover. Towards the end of the 19th century the two boiler insurance companies developed into insurers of boilers, engines, economisers, air receivers, surrounding property and the lives of employees and third parties. They also prepared specifications for new engines and boilers, and performed inspections and tests both during manufacture and in service.

In 1996 the descendants of the two first boiler insurance companies joined forces as the parent companies, *Royal Insurance and Sun Alliance*, merged in Britain's largest engineering insurance group, which has activities which include metallurgical, chemical and water treatment, non-destructive testing, and coverage of risks associated with computers and other electronic equipment.

Source: 'Royal and Sun Alliance Engineering: Enjoying an Honourable Heritage', *Foreword* magazine, August 1997, pp. 8–9.

it to assess the risks in advance: it will insure only if it has a satisfactory inspector's report. Moreover, because of the periodic inspection system, the insurer can also monitor how the insured company behaves: thus it can maintain a check on companies that shirk their responsibilities.

The state's role in this seems to be no more than a 'belt-and-braces' operation: a purely voluntary scheme in which companies would, out of self-interest, seek insurance and therefore be inspected would probably be just as effective. Indeed, engineering insurance grew up as such a voluntary scheme. However, the conclusion to be drawn is that in many circumstances a statutory inspection requirement is preferable to state prescription because it is more responsive to change.

The North Sea

The safety of offshore installations is a particularly complex issue. Nevertheless (or perhaps because it is so complex), the government is becoming less involved in the details of safety regulation.

After the disastrous accident in July 1988 on the Alpha installation of Occidental's Piper oilfield, when 167 people died, and the subsequent public inquiry report by Lord Cullen, the highly prescriptive safety régime in operation when the accident occurred – which had clearly been ineffective – was replaced. No longer were detailed requirements to be laid down for each offshore installation; instead, operators and owners were left to formulate their own safety plans ('safety cases') subject to acceptance by the Health and Safety Executive (HSE). Operators and owners could choose among six approved certifying authorities to carry out surveys of the installations.

In a more recent development, the government in 1996 introduced (over a two-year transitional period) a new form of verification. The operator or owner of an offshore installation still has to prepare a safety case which is subject to acceptance by the HSE but it is no longer a requirement to go to one of the six specified certifying authorities for surveys of the installation. Instead, the operator or owner makes his own identification of the critical elements in his safety case ('safety-critical elements') and finds his own 'independent and competent person' (for example, an electrical company or a pressure vessel specialist). Owners and operators therefore have some ability to set their own standards, subject to verification by a person they can choose provided he or she meets HSE definitions of 'independence' and 'competence'.[34]

Alcohol Self-Regulation in Britain

Suppliers of alcoholic drinks in Britain operate within a framework of licensing and regulation laid down by the state. But, within that framework, a system of voluntary regulation has developed, mainly through the Portman Group (a drinks-industry-funded body which aims to prevent mis-use of alcohol and to promote 'sensible drinking'). Consumer education campaigns, on television and elsewhere, some sponsored by the drinks industry, have helped cut the number of people killed or seriously injured by drink-drivers more in Britain than in most other countries – from 1,800 in 1980 to below 600 a year now. Other countries which have adopted government regulatory approaches have seen smaller declines. The United States, for instance, raised the minimum age for buying alcoholic drinks to 21; Australia introduced large-scale random breath tests; and in Scandinavia there are heavy fines and prison sentences.

To deal with the problem of under-age drinking, the Group introduced a Proof of Age card in 1990 to help both retailers (which are responsible for enforcing the law against purchases of alcoholic drink by under-18-year-olds) and legitimate purchasers who do not have a passport or other proof of age.

Another Portman Group initiative is aimed at reducing the confusion apparently caused by the launch of 'alcopops'. A Code of Practice on the Naming, Packaging and Merchandising of Alcoholic Drinks, introduced in April 1996 and revised in August 1997, is intended to avoid confusion between alcoholic and non-alcoholic drinks and to avoid any association between alcoholic drinks and anti-social behaviour. The Group operates an advisory

---

[34] The HSE's regulations explain how 'independence' and 'competence' are to be assessed: see *A Guide to the Installation, Verification and miscellaneous aspects of amendments by the Offshore Installation and Wells (Design and Construction etc.) Regulations 1996 to the Offshore Installations (Safety Case) Regulation 1992*, HSE Books, 1996, Regulations 7A, 7B, 7C and Schedule 9.

service so companies can obtain advance guidance on whether or not proposed products are likely to conform with the Code.

Voluntary Regulation in British Retailing

Large British retailers often appear to act beyond the requirements of government regulations. Some examples taken from the experience of Tesco, the largest supermarket group in Britain, are given in Box 2.

Turning to another country, New Zealand (which has been in the forefront of economic reform in many fields)[35] has moved to a much less prescriptive regulatory régime for transport, as explained in Box 3. A detailed system of transport regulation was replaced by one in which the government made members of the industry responsible for safety and concentrated on monitoring their compliance. The scheme appears to have enjoyed remarkable success, in terms of improved safety, lower costs of regulation and reduced prices.

12. The Case for More Voluntary Regulation

MORE EXAMPLES COULD BE GIVEN OF VOLUNTARY REGULATION which evidently works successfully or of areas where it could, with benefit, replace state regulation.[36] As one US study has pointed out:

> 'Regulation is usually identified with state or federal government, but that is a misconception. Today there are many independent third parties that privately regulate a sizeable portion of market activity without government involvement.'[37]

There are numerous different models. In some cases, the state provides a framework of regulation and companies in the industry form a self-regulatory organisation which fills in the details within that framework, avoiding the disadvantages of inflexible and highly prescriptive state rules. The Portman Group is an example of such a model.

In other cases, an industry is largely responsible for regulating its own activities but a statutory requirement exists for inspection (for example, by a 'competent person'). North Sea safety is one

---

[35] See Donald Brash, *New Zealand's Remarkable Reforms*, Occasional Paper No.100, London: Institute of Economic Affairs, 1996.

[36] For example, in the case of pensions, see David Simpson, *Regulating Pensions: Too Many Rules, Too Little Competition*, Hobart Paper No.131, London: Institute of Economic Affairs, 1996. In water, see Colin Robinson, 'Introducing Competition Into Water', in M. E. Beesley (ed.), *Regulating Utilities: Broadening the Debate*, Readings No.46, London: Institute of Economic Affairs, 1997.

[37] Yilmaz, *op.cit.*, p. 35.

Box 3

Transport in New Zealand

In New Zealand, public sector downsizing and deregulation in the transport sector have had remarkable and beneficial effects. For example, the Ministry of Transport once controlled all safety, price and licensing regulations for the trucking, shipping and airline industries. In 1991 the New Zealand government recognised that it was forcing taxpayers to pay for the delivery of quality and safety outcomes that should more properly have been borne by the industry. It therefore moved the bias of its transport safety regulatory scheme from one of operator compliance to operator accountability.

In practice, this move meant that the Ministry of Transport would no longer participate in the provision of safety outcomes; rather, it would simply ensure that the participants in the industry were doing so. The typical Ministry employee's day-to-day job changed from working for the transport providers to measuring their performance through regular monitoring, spot checks, and random visits.

While the Ministry's former task of providing safety personnel for the industry required 5,500 employees, its new mission of ensuring safe transport and monitoring performance required only 57 – about 1 per cent of the previous number. Despite this massive reduction in government regulators, the quality of the new regulatory scheme, and hence the objective measures of safety outcomes, improved across all the sectors of the industry. The quality and selection of the transport services have improved, and consumers have gained as prices for transport services have either stabilised or fallen since the 1980s.

This improvement in transport safety was not accidental. By making the transport industry pay for its own safety maintenance, the government gave those in the competitive market-place the incentive to regulate themselves as efficiently as possible. And, by measuring actual safety outcomes and performance rather than mere compliance with specific regulations, the Ministry returned to the industry the incentive to regulate itself effectively and responsibly as it discovered more innovative approaches to providing safe transport.

Thus by scrutinising its functions, focusing on measurable results, and restructuring its regulatory scheme, the Ministry of Transport was able to perform more effectively its job of reducing the number of accidents and lives lost – and at a fraction of the previous cost to taxpayers.

Source: James M. Buchanan Center for Political Economy, George Mason University, Fairfax, Virginia, private communication.

such example. Another is engineering insurance, except that it grew up as a voluntary system policed by insurance companies and it still seems to operate mainly because of the involvement of insurance companies: inspection and insurance are part of an integrated system.

There are also examples (such as Underwriters Laboratories) where regulation is entirely carried out by the private sector. That is, a system of regulation has emerged naturally in response to the demands of producers and consumers and provides standard-setting by independent parties as well as compliance procedures (testing, certification, and so on).

The great advantage of the systems which have emerged naturally is that they avoid many of the practical difficulties of government regulation set out earlier in this paper. Because the costs of regulation are not external to the regulatory bodies, the tendency towards over-regulation which exists in state systems is avoided. Furthermore, the system is more readily adaptable to changing circumstances than state regulation normally is. As explained in Section 8, one of the principal costs of state regulation (though an 'invisible' cost) is the dampening effect on entre-preneurship and innovation which stems from the rigid rules usually associated with government regulation.

The greater flexibility of private systems is a major advantage. Moreover, the ability of markets to produce incentives to act safely and sensibly is not generally recognised. For example, one of the authors was recently purchasing car insurance for a vehicle for which the principal driver would be his teenage son. The insurance broker asked for a copy of the son's latest school report. Noting excellent grades in all subjects, a significant discount was offered. A further discount is also available for the successful completion of a driver's education course. A photocopy of the school report and proof of completion of the driver's course are then forwarded with all other relevant paperwork to the insurance company by the broker: the discount for good grades is slightly greater than that for completing the driving course. The market is clearly making very fine and subtle distinctions of the sort that regulation simply cannot handle.

Finally, in this context, it is worth pondering what would happen if the driving licence system in the UK was privatised. At the moment, the young 17-year-old learner driver is handed a licence valid for 53 years – that is, until the driver's 70th birthday. There is no further retraining or re-education and little if any incentive to hone skills other than a jump in insurance premiums charged following a claim. With licensing in private hands, perhaps even run by the insurers, one would expect a great deal of experimentation to go on, with a number of different refresher courses emerging. It is also inconceivable that the private sector would issue a licence for over 50 years.

13. Conclusions

An American study of regulation concluded: '... there is a huge world of private regulation that regulators, members of Congress, the president, and journalists are oblivious to.'[38] The same is probably true in Britain, though in both countries private regulation must have been crowded out by government regulation. At the least, the extent of private regulation and its effects should be studied: in Britain it would be an appropriate task for the Better Regulation Task Force and the new Regulatory Impact Unit[39] since voluntary regulation seems to have inherent advantages over the state variety. Government regulation seems frequently to be ineffective in achieving its stated aims, compliance costs are often high and it discourages enterprise. Too often it appears as a large and expensive sledgehammer which misses a relatively small nut.

There are four additional steps which we would recommend. They are set out below, ranked from the least radical to the most radical:

- Impose on other government-appointed regulators the duty to promote competition which now applies to the utility regulators (or a duty with similar impact) in order to curb the expansionary tendencies of regulatory bodies.

- Transfer monitoring and compliance procedures (inspection, testing and certification) wherever possible away from

---

[38] Yilmaz, *op.cit.*, p. 32.

[39] 'Brussels to be targeted in drive to curb red tape', *The Financial Times,* 28 April 1999, describes the new British arrangements for assessing the impact of regulation.

government regulators to the private sector. For example, a state requirement for inspection by a 'competent person' (as in the engineering insurance and North Sea cases) could replace prescriptive rules. The state would require regulation but would not set detailed standards nor be involved directly in compliance procedures.

• Permit private companies to set standards (possibly in competition with existing government regulators); and

• Make compliance with privately-set standards voluntary so that private regulation retains its non-coercive character. Producers could decide whether or not to opt in to compliance with particular standards, depending on whether or not they appeared to enhance reputation. One of the factors in consumers' purchasing decisions would be their assessment of the value of particular standards.

These recommendations should appeal to governments in many countries which are concerned about the effects of regulation and have come to recognise its dangers. The costs of government regulation are such that there is a *prima facie* case for replacing much of it by voluntary regulation in the interests of improving economic performance. Furthermore, many of the problems which government regulation is intended to solve would be better dealt with by voluntary means. Whether it is a matter of improving health and safety, safeguarding the environment, providing favourable terms and conditions of work, promoting good practice in selling financial products, or addressing the other issues at which government regulation is directed, there is a strong case for arguing that the way forward should be through voluntary action.

COMMENTARY:
MARKETS AND REGULATION
Norman Barry

NOTWITHSTANDING THE COLLAPSE OF ECONOMIC PLANNING and most types of central control, the state continues to cause nearly as much havoc with the private market as it did under the more familiar nationalisation methods of old. Just as there are many ways to skin a cat, so there are innumerable devices for hampering, if not completely disabling, the private enterprise system. Despite constant pledges by governments of all stripes to relieve transactors from the regulatory morass, consumers and producers face over 3,000 new regulations a year; a figure which has changed little, except to worsen, in the past decade. In their new publication, John Blundell and Colin Robinson lucidly explain the reasons for the rise of the regulatory state and suggest feasible alternatives. As they point out,[1] the absence of state regulation does not mean that there is a regulatory void, that helpless consumers are at the mercy of predatory producers unconstrained by any rules: on the contrary, the market will generate its own practices which will be more effective in protecting consumers than the prevailing set of state *prescriptions*. Such action does not depend on a change in the motivations of producers, it is in their self-interest to provide high standards of safety and to protect the environment. It is the believers in state, compulsory regulation who require some change in the human personality; they hope that the regulators themselves will not become opportunists, rent-seekers and empire-builders, that they will pursue the 'public interest' without the usual incentives provided by the market. Blundell and Robinson have produced an admirable summary and penetrating critique of the current regulatory

---

[1] *Regulation Without the State*, London: IEA, Occasional Paper 109, p. 13 (p. 1 of this Readings).

regime; they have also made cogent suggestions as to how much of regulation can be returned to the market (where it actually began). All I can do here is to add to their suggestions and explore further some of the themes they have introduced.

The Market as the Best Regulator

DESPITE THE FACT THAT WESTERN LIBERAL CAPITALIST ECONOMIES are the most prosperous *and* least harmful production systems in history, the public is particularly prone to panics and scares over such things as hygiene, food safety and product reliability. In Britain we have experienced this in no small measure with the alleged 'crises' over eggs, BSE and other headline-grabbing incidents but as Christopher Booker[2] has tirelessly and assiduously documented, most of the regulations designed to allay the public's fears have in fact been counter-productive; they have actually made matters worse and we would live in a more secure environment if the matter had been left to private enterprise. Indeed, many of the punitive legal actions taken against producers are based on the flimsiest of scientific evidence and are provoked by people with the most to gain from over-regulation. They are normally activists (such as Greenpeace, which has a record of lawlessness and contempt for scientific knowledge in its campaign over the environment[3]), regulatory bureaucrats who secure significant rents from hypergovernment activity and potential litigants who gain financially from persecuting corporations.

The current campaign against genetically modified food is a good example of activism. There is actually no scientific evidence that it causes health problems: indeed modifications to 'natural' foods have been going on since the beginning of agriculture and genetically modified food has environmental advantages in addition to the higher productivity it generates. It has, of course, been practised in the US, surely the most safety conscious country in the world, for a considerable length of time. Again the campaign has been conducted with no respect for the law or for property

---

[2] Christopher Booker, 'The Regulatory Crisis of the 1990s – the Problem', *Economic Affairs*, 14 (June 1994), pp. 18–22.

[3] See M. Neal and C. Davies, *The Corporation Under Siege*, London: Social Affairs Unit, 1998, pp. 22–25.

rights. Even farmers who have been conducting genuine scientific research into the techniques, something which should be welcomed by the activists, have been attacked. They are, of course, demanding more government regulation when it is the producers of genetically modified food who are doing the appropriate research. The first point to stress in this is that the market itself (and the not undemanding assumption that consumers are rational) is the best safety-enhancing mechanism. The success of capitalist economies is not to be measured solely by their ability to produce wanted goods and services but by the rise in standards brought about by competition.[4] In Wildavsky's famous phrase, 'wealth means more health'. This is not a tribute to the morality of capitalists, which we can assume is no different from anybody else's, but to the mechanics of the exchange system. There is simply no money in unsafe products.

In Wildavsky's theory, we should not chase the illusion of a completely risk-free society. If we do that we would prohibit many wealth-enhancing activities and so deplete the resources that would otherwise be available for combating hazards. In fact, his argument is that, ultimately, safety is improved by the taking of risks since that allows for the build-up of knowledge which is essential for dealing with a necessarily uncertain world. Such knowledge is accumulated by the trial and error process of the market. The safety of the whole depends on some unsafety in the parts. Thus the requirement of some government regulations, that the elimination of all potential risk be demonstrated, can actually cause more harm in the long run. What we should not try to do is anticipate all future catastrophes (which is impossible) but learn from the past.

A good example of a government agency actually causing harm is the American Food and Drug Administration (especially under its zealous erstwhile commissioner, David Kessler) which has delayed and forbidden many medications because they could not be proved to be absolutely safe. The most striking case was the banning of Opren, the anti-arthritic drug, in 1982, because of side effects which could not be clearly linked to the drug. How many people have died, or suffered, because of such regulation? The removal of

---

4 A. Wildavsky, *Searching for Safety*, New Brunswick: Transaction, 1988.

33

'untested' drugs from the market is a good example of what Blundell and Robinson[5] accurately call the 'invisible' costs of government regulation.

Why Government Involvement?

IF THE MARKET IS SO GOOD AT CORRECTING ERRORS and providing the right incentives for health and safety, why has the state become so concerned? As Blundell and Robinson[6] correctly observe, it is a combination of virtuous but mistaken economic theory by well-meaning reformers and ignoble opportunism by selfish bureaucrats. The mistaken theory derives from the doctrine of 'market failure'; because of ignorance on the part of consumers and 'externalities' in trade, the market might not produce an optimum, in our case the 'correct' amount of safety. But the main point here is that markets are always to some extent imperfect and it is the continual process of experimentation, guided by prices, that gradually pushes the exchange system to an optimum, albeit temporary and subject to incessant change. It would be a very optimistic theorist who assumed that an imperfect state, controlled by utility maximisers (officials) much less constrained by price, could significantly improve on this.

But worse, it is a fallacy to assume that government officials are disinterested purveyors of the public interest. They are themselves personally interested, in terms of salary and career prospects, in the outcome of the regulatory process. As Blundell and Robinson show, the bulk of the costs of regulation are borne by the regulated and not by government. The externalities here are quite surprising.[7] Is it any wonder that the regulation significantly exceeds an 'efficient' level when it costs so little for government and its officials gain so much from it? There is little that can moderate the supply since the regulations are, at best, passed by a democratic assembly which, subject to crude majority rule procedures, cannot be relied on to generate the genuine public interest, or control the regulatory mania.

---

[5] *Regulation Without the State*, pp. 16–18 (pp. 4–6 of this Readings).

[6] *Regulation Without the State*, pp. 15–16 (pp. 2–4 of this Readings).

[7] *Regulation Without the State*, pp. 17–21 (pp. 5–9 of this Readings).

It is, though, even worse than this since most of the regulations that so disable entrepreneurship and discourage innovation are normally passed as statutory instruments, under pre-existing Acts, and are subject to little examination; even if representatives had the time or the incentive to enquire into their rationale there is little opportunity to oppose them. They are, of course, ignorant and a prey to officials who can easily persuade them of the scientific necessity of some arbitrary rule. It is only when the effects of such rules become widely known that representatives are made aware of them, and then it is too late. The classic example here is the complex and costly arrangements for abattoirs, impelled in part, but not entirely, by European law, which have crippled the UK animal slaughter industry. As Christopher Booker has sedulously chronicled, British law often exceeds European requirements. The prevailing attitude to any problem is that 'something must be done' and that the state is the automatic institution to do it. Politicians are always likely to respond to the aforementioned 'panics' over particular issues that catch the public eye and are less likely to take a reasoned view.

Allied to this is a further stimulation to regulation: the habit of referring to particular newsworthy cases of a faulty product or dangerous procedure rather than looking at the overall, or average, figures; personalities make better news than statistics. So many pieces of oppressive regulation are responses to *particular* events. Presumably it is these events that have given rise to the 'precautionary principle', which holds that restrictions, even when not fully justified scientifically, should be enforced because, in our ignorance, we cannot be sure of the future. But this constant concern with tomorrow, and less emphasis on what we can learn from the past, would not merely put a stop to all progress, it would make the world a more dangerous place.

Equally disturbing is the fact that regulations almost always turn out to be irreversible. This permanence is explicable using the arguments of Blundell and Robinson[8] which show how small minorities gain significantly from regulation while the vast apathetic majority loses just a little. Just as the former have a great incentive to organise and press for more government rules, they

---

[8] *Regulation Without the State*, pp. 21–22 (pp. 9–10 of this Readings).

make real gains from their retention, regardless of the adverse effects on society as a whole. All government attempts to 'make a bonfire of controls' come up against this problem. The protectors of the existing regulatory regime can capitalise on the illusion that the restrictions have made the world a safer place.

What is significant from a philosophical, as well as a practical, point of view is the increasing tendency to put demands for more regulation, especially over things like safety at work and the claim for a perfectly harmless product, in the form of indefeasible 'rights', that is, claims that must be honoured whatever the circumstances and the costs. This is a view that has some plausibility in relation to the basic human rights, for example for a fair trial, free speech and so on but it is little more than a rhetorical device in regulatory matters. The point is that here the claims have to be assessed alongside other important demands, say, of efficiency or utility. The pleas for more regulation are in reality little more than claims for the protection of *interests* – which have to be put alongside other interests that clamour for satisfaction from the political system. This new language of rights functions as an 'argument stopper' which excludes all other equally valid considerations in policy formulation; demonstration of the malign consequences of regulation is automatically excluded from the debate. But the rights talk is selective; for instance, in the debate about the environment little cognisance is taken of *property* rights; they may be validated in positive law and their enforcement could well make regulation here irrelevant. Neither is any reference made to the loss in economic freedom that state action involves.

It is convincingly argued by Blundell and Robinson that the differential impact that regulation has on the members of economic groups determines its extent, up to a point.[9] Big business is likely to favour extensive controls and restrictions because it can cope with the additional costs, though the new rules raise entry costs for rivals. In the US especially, regulatory bodies are likely to be 'captured' by those whom they regulate, guaranteeing the triumph of producer over consumer interests.

One of the early attempts at labour regulation in the US was the New York state statute (1905) that limited the amount of hours per

---

[9] *Regulation Without the State*, pp. 23–24 (pp. 11–12 of this Readings).

week bakers could work. It was originally struck down by the Supreme Court as unconstitutional,[10] but the economically interesting aspect of the case was that the statute was the product of pressure group activity by a combination of big New York bakers fearing competition from immigrants prepared to work much longer hours. It is worth noting that now, unlike in the early part of the twentieth century, individuals and minorities will get no help from the Supreme Court if they challenge regulatory legislation.

What is to Be Done?

AS BLUNDELL AND ROBINSON CONSTANTLY STRESS, the present regulatory systems are anti-competitive, inefficient and costly, but they also show that the state is actually a latecomer to the scene (as it was for welfare). Markets had always spontaneously developed, in the interests of traders, complex rules and practices which protected the consumer. Indeed, the beginnings of commercial law are in the Law Merchant which was very efficient (so much so that it was captured by the rent-seeking common lawyers in the seventeenth century). As in welfare, once the state arrived it crowded out private regulation. But, nevertheless, there is still a considerable amount of private regulation and this could form the basis of regulation without the state.

Blundell and Robinson record, in stimulating detail, just how much market-generated regulation there has always been. Furthermore, these rules have worked hand in hand with private insurance to provide as much security as the state, if not more. It certainly comes at lower cost. Even now there is an impressive range of self-regulatory market devices in Britain and the US: most of these rules are aimed at protecting the consumer from faulty and dangerous goods. It is interesting that Blundell and Robinson devote considerable attention to the development of insurance and inspection for potentially hazardous equipment, such as steam boilers in the nineteenth century. Such is the flexibility of private arrangements that they can generate quick responses to any change in production methods. By contrast, the state is slow and cumbersome. Modern and highly prescriptive safety legislation could not prevent the

---

[10] The case was *Lochner v. York* in which the Court upheld a right to contract. The constitutionality of this was always doubted though the economics was correct.

Piper oilfield disaster in 1988, and because of this tragedy the operators have been permitted some freedom in their choice of regulatory regime and can employ private companies to guarantee it.[11] Although such schemes are subject to ultimate verification by the Health and Safety Executive there is considerable liberty for operators to choose safety methods. There is a fatal cast of mind that assumes that because a system conforms to a national compulsory standard it must be safe.

The danger in the US, however, is that because of the dominance of tort law there it is becoming impossible for people to contract their way out of liability; thus, no matter how many warning signs are erected and safety devices installed, a producer might still be liable for damage caused. The Dow Corning Company was driven into liquidation because many women claimed that their health was damaged by breast implants made by the company, even though there was absolutely no genuine scientific evidence to support this. To free modern society from coercive regulation requires that citizens be treated as responsible agents capable of making rational choices; something the modern state is reluctant to do.

An area not considered by Blundell and Robinson which has been subjected to excessive state regulation is finance. There is a myriad of controls and regulations in stock markets which are designed to protect unwary small investors from well-informed and skilful operators. The most obvious example are the regulations designed to outlaw insider dealing.[12] As is well known, they do not eliminate it; the phenomenon always occurs (there is indeed, an economic justification for it) but the imposition of strict rules has two malign consequences:

- First, the big profits go to the really unscrupulous.

- Second, the effect of the regulation is to deter honest market analysts who run the risk of becoming insiders, and subject to criminal law', if they discover and act on hitherto undisclosed information.

---

[11] *Regulation Without the State*, p. 35 (p. 23 of this Readings).

[12] N. Barry, *Insider Dealing*, London: Foundation for Business Responsibility, 1996.

Such rules simply coagulate the flow of information in the market. The correct solution to the alleged problem was recommended by Richard Epstein:

> for a company to legitimise insider trading all it needs is a provision in its charter saying: 'if you want to deal in the shares of this company, please understand that every employee and every director is entitled to trade on inside information to their heart's content. If you do not want to trade with us you are free to buy shares in our competitor which does not allow that option.[13]

We must rid ourselves of the meretricious and vacuous ideal, so beloved by regulators, of a 'level playing field' in securities markets.

Conclusion

THERE IS MUCH TO LEARN ABOUT MARKETS and regulation in Blundell and Robinson's stimulating paper. As always, there is more to add. As a general principle I would recommend that we extend the idea of competition further than our authors do. What about markets in political institutions? Political boundaries are more or less fixed in stable liberal democracies but that does not mean the limits of political authority are immutable. For it is surely conceivable to introduce freedom in regulatory regimes by delegating authority to decentralised political units and expanding the opportunities for citizens to move to one of their choice. Most regulations, especially those to do with the environment, are nationwide and compulsory, but if lower units of government were free to compete in a market for regulation it would probably produce lighter burdens and the rules could be adjusted to fit local circumstances. Why should emission standards be the same in Los Angeles as in Montana? Only because the state says so.

It does not mean that political units would be engaged in a race to the bottom in order to attract more citizens. For as living standards rise people will demand cleaner air, more commodious streets and a more attractive environment. But that is no reason why poorer areas, in need of investment and employment, should not be able to offer

---

[13] R. Epstein, *The Concealment: Use and Disclosure of Information,* Wellington: New Zealand Business Round Table, p. 17.

39

a lighter regulatory regime. However, the state will only offer such variety if it is compelled to do so by the market. A start could be made by turning the European Union into a genuine *confederal* organisation within which member states could compete with each other over regulation. At the moment each is subjected to uniform rules.

COMMENTARY:

THE BENEFITS OF PRIVATE REGULATION
David Boaz

THE WORLD IS A COMPLEX PLACE. Most of us seek more certainty in at least some aspects of our lives than might seem to occur naturally. Especially in modern market societies, many of us have tried to achieve certainty, security, or stability through regulation. What is often not understood, as John Blundell and Colin Robinson explain in *Regulation Without the State,* is that much of the 'regulation' that improves our lives is not coercive or government-created but rather voluntary and the product of market decision-making. Indeed, the most important fact about private regulation is how pervasive it is in our lives, and how unaware of it we are most of the time.

Indeed, private systems that offer us some assurance of safety, quality, or other values take an amazing variety of forms: Better Business Bureaus, *Consumer Reports,* codes of professional responsibility, bond rating services, *Zagat's Survey* of American restaurants, Underwriters Laboratories, kosher certifiers, brand names, franchises, private communities, and more.

In political discourse today, 'regulation' is assumed to refer to government rules, the violation of which will result in legal penalties such as fines or even incarceration. But the original meaning of 'regulate' was 'to make regular'. That is the sense in which the US Constitution authorises Congress to 'regulate commerce ... among the several states.' Much of the political struggle in modern capitalist countries is over the extent of government regulation. But often the real issue at hand is not whether a particular activity will be regulated but whether it will be regulated coercively, by the state, or voluntarily, through private actions.

Charles Murray urges readers of his book *What It Means to Be a Libertarian* to imagine a law that would allow individual businesses to opt out of the entire system of state regulation. The only requirement would be that stores and manufacturers opting out of regulation would have to display large signs reading UNREGULATED. 'Businesses that choose to remain within the regulatory system are free to display equally prominent signs reading something like, "This business proudly complies with all government regulations."'[1] But of course, as Murray recognises, it would be more fair and accurate for almost all the 'unregulated' firms to be labelled 'regulated by [various private entities and systems]' than 'unregulated'.

In her paper on the subject[2] and in this volume, Yesim Yilmaz discusses some of the advantages of private regulation, notably its flexible, responsive, and dynamic character. Private regulation, driven by the needs of firms and customers, is much more able to change when it becomes either too permissive or too restrictive or when technological or other changes demand new rules.

In this comment I want to touch on some specific examples of private regulation.

Brand Names

BRAND NAMES ARE ALL AROUND US, yet we often forget how useful they are in finding high-quality products. Economist Daniel Klein offers an example:

> Suppose the muffler drops off your car in the middle of Iowa. You pull off the interstate and find Joe's Auto Repair. The mechanics at Joe's see that you are from out of state. They know that, regardless of how fairly they treat you, you will not be returning and will not be speaking to other potential customers. Hence, caution is advised. Then you notice a Meineke shop down the road. You will never be returning to that Meineke shop either, but for some reason you have more trust in Meineke.
>
> Although you will never return to that particular Meineke shop, you might reach a judgment about Meineke shops in general on the basis of your experience at that shop. The franchisee at that shop doesn't

---

[1] Charles Murray, *What It Means to Be a Libertarian: A Personal Interpretation*, New York: Broadway, 1997, p. 64.

[2] Yesim Yilmaz, 'Private Regulation: A Real Alternative for Regulatory Reform', Washington, DC: Cato Institute, Policy Analysis no. 303, 20 April 1998.

care whether you ever go to another Meineke shop, but the parent company does. The parent company wants that franchisee to treat you fairly, and it takes steps to make that happen. Meineke employs 'mystery shoppers' who pose as ordinary consumers with broken cars. Also, the parent company receives and remedies customer complaints. Consumers might not be consciously aware of such trust-building practices, but they rightly intuit that some kind of assurance lies in familiarity. The company name is a bit like a friend, and the serviceman wearing the company logo is like the friend of a friend. He is not your bridge to Meineke; Meineke is your bridge to him.[3]

Kenneth D. Walker, president and CEO of Meineke, writes that Klein underestimates Meineke's efforts to ensure good service by each of its franchisees:

Beyond the training, the resources, and the codified procedures we provide, the *Meineke System* provides numerous incentives for dealers to deliver quality to *every* Meineke customer. So in your hypothetical case where a Meineke dealer in the middle of Iowa spies your out-of-state license, he may not 'care whether you ever go to another Meineke shop', but there are solid reasons why he *should*.

Here are a couple of the primary reasons:

1 A fixed percentage of *every* Meineke sale goes into *national advertising,* which means that subsequent business conducted by a Meineke customer in New York City *does* substantially benefit the dealer in Iowa City....

2 If the above math seems a bit abstract for the average Meineke dealer, our *Intershop System* is more down-to-earth. Linked to our nationwide warranty, our intershop system makes the original shop responsible for parts and service quality *no matter where* a customer might present his or her warranty. So if that replaced muffler drops off again between Cedar Rapids and the Bowery, our New York City shop calls up that Iowa City shop and requests repayment....

So throughout the Meineke chain, if our dealers wish to remain in good standing with the Home Office and their peers – or if they're

---

[3] Daniel B. Klein, 'How Trust Is Achieved in Free Markets', Washington, DC: *Cato Policy Report,* November–December 1997.

blessed with enlightened self-interest – we do think our franchisees 'care whether you ever go to another Meineke shop'.[4]

Meineke and other franchises care very much about their nationwide quality and create elaborate systems – which we could call regulation – to ensure that customers get uniformly good products and services. Retail stores have a similar investment in their reputations, so they also seek to guarantee high quality in the products they sell. Sears, Roebuck and Co., a pioneer in retail catalogue sales that now operates almost 3,000 stores, has been testing the products it sells since 1911. Its Sears Quality Evaluation Center in Chicago encompasses 33,000 square feet. 'There's nothing we can't build here,' says director Dave Macarus, 'or break.' Sears tests and sells all the products carrying its own labels (such as Craftsman and Weedwacker) and many of the products it sells under the manufacturer's name. A staff of more than 50 employees conducts about 400 evaluations a month. According to a *Washington Post* report,

> For many evaluations there is no precedent, government standard or easily measurable criteria such as pounds of pressure per square inch. That's when the technicians … have to be inventive.

They have to decide what the standard should be for a product and how to test to that standard. 'At the Sears lab, experience and common sense bring at least as much to bear on product safety as dry, technical standards' – which might be one difference between flexible private systems and rigid, codified state systems.[5]

Insurance

IN A MARKET SOCIETY, insurance is one of the best regulators. Consumers carry insurance in case they get harmed. Firms carry insurance in case they get sued. In each case the insurance company has a strong incentive to know what liability it is assuming. Insurance companies sometimes deny liability coverage for products that lack the Underwriters Laboratories label. They impose requirements on homebuilders and other firms.

---

[4] Kenneth D. Walker, President and CEO, Meineke, letter to Daniel B. Klein, 22 April 1999.

[5] 'Making the Grade: Between New Product and Consumer, Sears Puts 33,000 Square Feet of Testing Lab', *Washington Post,* 18 January 1996, Home Section, p. T10.

People have often thought that insurance is a valuable service for government to provide. Many of the largest federal programmes are intended to insure Americans against economic and other risks: Social Security, Medicare and Medicaid, deposit insurance, flood insurance, and more. The general argument for insurance is that a loss that would be disastrous for a single individual can be absorbed by a large group of similarly situated individuals. We pool our money in an insurance plan to guard against the small possibility of a catastrophic event.

The argument for government insurance, as opposed to competitive private insurers, is that you can spread the risk over a larger number of people. But as George L. Priest of the Yale Law School points out, government insurance has had many unfortunate results. There's no economic advantage to creating an insurance pool larger than necessary, and there are definite disadvantages to large monopolies. Government is very bad at charging risk-appropriate premiums, so its insurance tends to be too expensive for risk-averse people and too cheap for those who engage in high-risk activities. And government dramatically compounds the 'moral hazard' problem – that is, the tendency of people who have insurance to take more risks. Insurance companies try to control this by having deductibles and copayments, so the insured will still face some loss beyond what insurance covers, and by excluding certain kinds of activities from coverage (like suicide or behaviour that is more risky than the insurance pool is designed for). For both economic and political reasons, government usually doesn't employ such tools, so it actually encourages more risk.

Priest cites several specific examples:

- Federal savings-and-loan insurance increased the risk level of investments; the savings-and-loan companies would reap the profits from high-risk ventures, but the taxpayers would make up the losses, so why not go for the big return?

- Government-provided unemployment insurance increases both the extent and the duration of unemployment; people would find new jobs sooner if they didn't have unemployment insurance, or if their own insurance rates were affected by how much they used, as car insurance rates are.

- Priest writes, 'I will not go so far as to claim that government-provided insurance increases the frequency of natural disasters. On the other hand, I have no doubt whatsoever that the government provision of insurance increases the magnitude of *losses* from natural disasters.' Flood insurance, for instance, provided by the US government at less than the market price, encourages more building on flood plains and on the fragile barrier islands off the East Coast.

The desire to reduce one's exposure to risk is natural, and markets provide people with means to that end. But when people sought to reduce risk through government insurance programmes, the result was to channel resources toward *more* risky activities and thus to increase the level of risk and the level of losses suffered by the whole society.

Still, the market has provided many opportunities for people to choose the level of risk with which they are comfortable. Many kinds of insurance are available. Different investments – stocks, bonds, mutual funds, certificates of deposit – allow people to balance risk versus return in a way they prefer. Farmers can reduce their risks by selling their expected harvest before it comes in, locking in a price. They're protected against falling prices, though they lose the opportunity to make big profits from rising prices. Commodities futures markets give farmers and others the opportunity to hedge against price shifts. Many people don't understand commodities and futures markets, or even the simpler securities markets; in Tom Wolfe's novel *The Bonfire of the Vanities,* the bond trader Sherman McCoy thought of himself as a Master of the Universe but couldn't explain to his daughter the value of what he did. Politicians and popular writers rail against 'paper entrepreneurs' or 'money changers', but those mysterious markets not only guide capital to projects where it will best serve consumer demand, they also help millions of Americans to regulate their risks.

A new twist for farmers is the opportunity to contract with food processors to grow specific crops. More than 90% of vegetables are now grown under production contracts, along with smaller percentages of other crops.[6] The contracts give farmers less independence but also less risk, which many of them prefer.

---

[6] Barnaby J. Feder, 'Putting Farmers on a Contract', *New York Times,* 20 May 1995, p. 37.

Meanwhile, major commodities markets like the Chicago Board of Trade, the Chicago Mercantile Exchange, and the New York Mercantile Exchange are looking for new investment options to offer to customers. In 1996 the Chicago Merc began offering milk price futures – allowing people to lock in milk prices, or bet on price shifts – in response to deregulation, which will likely mean lower but fluctuating prices. The Nymex established a market in electricity futures, which will come in handy as electric utilities are deregulated.[7]

The Board of Trade is one of the players looking for new ways to protect insurance companies – and by extension everyone who buys insurance or invests in insurance companies – from the threat posed by megadisasters. According to the *New York Times,* two of the most destructive natural disasters in American history have occurred in the past few years: Hurricane Andrew in 1992, which cost insurers $16 billion in South Florida, and the 1994 Los Angeles earthquake, which cost $11 billion.[8] (Note that the reason these were the 'most destructive' disasters ever is that Americans own more wealth than ever, so financial losses are greater.) Insurers fear a disaster of $50 billion magnitude, which could put insurance companies out of business and even be too much for the reinsurance business, which sells policies to protect insurers from large losses. They are looking for new ways to pool the risk, including catastrophe futures on the Board of Trade, with which insurers could hedge against the possibility of large losses. Investors would make money by, in effect, betting that there would be no such catastrophe.

Reinsurers are also offering 'act of God' bonds that would pay very high interest but would require bondholders to forgo repayment in the event of disaster. Catastrophe futures and 'act of God' bonds will help keep insurance coverage available and reasonably priced. They also raise the question: If the market can adequately deal with even the prospect of multibillion-dollar financial disasters, precisely what services can government supply better than the market?

---

[7] Barnaby J. Feder, 'In Search of New Commodities', *New York Times,* 15 March 1996, p. C1.

[8] Michael Quint, 'New Tools Spread Risks of Insurers', *New York Times,* 15 May 1995, p. A1.

Private Communities

ONE AREA WHERE PEOPLE SEEK SAFETY and stability is in their residential environment. Some Americans move far from cities so they won't have to deal with externalities created by other people. Others have turned to zoning and other forms of state regulation to try to regulate their surroundings. Recently another approach has become widespread in the US: some 4 million Americans have chosen to live in some 30,000 private, gated communities. Another 24 million live in locked condominiums, cooperatives, or apartment houses, which are small gated communities, and as many as 42 million live in community associations, some of which are not gated. Why do people choose to live in private communities? The first answer is, to protect themselves from crime and the dramatic deterioration of public services in many large cities. A college professor complains in the *Washington Post* about 'the new Middle Ages . . . a kind of medieval landscape in which defensible, walled and gated towns dot the countryside.' People built walls around their cities in the Middle Ages to protect themselves from bandits and marauders, and many Americans are making the same choice.

Private communities are a peaceful but comprehensive response to the failure of big government. Like their federal counterpart, local governments today tax us more heavily than ever but offer deteriorating services in return. Not only do police seem unable to combat rising crime, but the schools get worse and worse, garbage and litter don't get picked up, potholes aren't fixed, panhandlers confront us on every corner. Private communities can provide physical safety for their residents, partly by excluding from the community people who are neither residents nor guests.

But there's a broader reason for choosing to live in a private community. Local governments can't satisfy the needs and preferences of all their residents. People have different preferences in terms of population density, housing types, the presence of children, and so on. Rules that might cater to some citizens' preferences would be unconstitutional or offensive to the freewheeling spirit of other citizens.

Private communities can solve some of these public goods problems. In the larger developments, the homes, the streets, the sewers, the parklands are all private. After buying a house or condominium there, residents pay a monthly fee that covers security, maintenance, and management. Many of the communities are both gated and guarded.

Many have rules that would range from annoying to infuriating to unconstitutional if imposed by a government – regulations on house colours, shrubbery heights, on-street parking, even gun ownership. People choose such communities partly because they find the rules, even strict rules, congenial.

Economists Donald J. Boudreaux and Randall G. Holcombe offer a theoretical explanation for the growing popularity of private communities, which they call contractual governments. Having constitutional rules drawn up by a single developer, who then offers the property and the rules as a package to buyers, reduces the decision-making costs of developing appropriate rules and allows people to choose communities on the basis of the kind of rules they offer. The desire to make money is a strong incentive for the developer to draw up good rules.

Boudreaux and Holcombe write,

> The establishment of a contractual government appears to be the closest thing to a real-world social contract that can be found because it is created behind something analogous to a veil [of ignorance], and because everyone unanimously agrees to move into the contractual government's jurisdiction.[9]

Fred Foldvary points out that most 'public goods' exist within a particular space, so the goods can be provided only to people who rent or purchase access to the space. That allows entrepreneurs to overcome the problem of people trying to 'free-ride' off others' payments for public goods. Entrepreneurs try to make their space attractive to customers by supplying the best possible combination of characteristics, which will vary from space to space. Foldvary points out that private communities, shopping centres, industrial parks, theme parks, and hotel interiors are all private spaces created by entrepreneurs, who have a much better incentive than governments to discover and respond to consumer demand. And

---

[9] Donald J. Boudreaux and Randall G. Holcombe, 'Government by Contract', *Public Finance Quarterly* 17 no. 3 (July 1989), p. 275.

many private entrepreneurs competing for business can supply a much wider array of choices than governments will.[10]

Private communities – including condominiums and apartment buildings – come in virtually unlimited variety. Prices vary widely, as does the general level of amenities. Some have policies banning children, pets, guns, garish colours, rentals or whatever else might be perceived to reduce residents' enjoyment of the space. The growing 'cohousing' movement responds to the need many people feel for a closer sense of community by offering living spaces centred around a common house for group meals and activities. Some people create cohousing arrangements based on a shared religious commitment.

Shopping malls might also be considered both private communities and private regulatory systems. Malls try to provide shoppers with a more pleasant experience than traditional on-street stores can offer. Their advantages include the proximity of many stores, protection from the weather, cleanliness and protection from crime and disruptive behaviour. As governments become less able to supply clean, peaceful, pleasant city streets, people increasingly choose private malls that offer what customers seek. Because they are private, malls are more responsive to consumer demand. They can require that stores contribute to general maintenance, decoration and security; and stores are happy to do so because they find that their money is spent efficiently on services that benefit them. Also because they are private, malls can exclude from their premises people who don't abide by bourgeois standards of behaviour. Mall security officers rarely have to eject anyone; the mere knowledge that they *could* do so is usually enough to encourage proper behaviour by visitors. Suburban malls seem to

---

[10] Fred Foldvary, *Public Goods and Private Communities*, Aldershot: Edward Elgar, 1994. Most books on private communities are more critical. See, for example, Evan McKenzie, *Privatopia: Homeowner Associations and the Rise of Residential Private Government*, New Haven: Yale University Press, 1994; Edward J. Blakely and Mary Gail Snyder, *Fortress America: Gated Communities in the US*, Washington, DC: Brookings Institution Press, 1997; and two new books on the Walt Disney Co.'s attempt to create a new community: Andrew Ross, *The Celebration Chronicles: Life, Liberty and the Pursuit of Property Values in Disney's New Town*, New York: Ballantine, 1999, and Douglas Frantz and Catherine Collins, *Celebration, USA: Living in Disney's Brave New Town*, New York: Henry Holt, 1999. See also David Boaz, 'Gates of Wrath: Angry about Crime, People Have Good Reason to Fence Out the World', *Washington Post,* 7 January 1996, p. C1.

assume that standards of behaviour are within the implicit knowledge of their customers. An urban mall near my office in Washington, DC, makes the rules explicit (see box).

Private communities are a vital part of civil society. They give more people an opportunity to find the kinds of living (or working, or shopping, or entertainment) arrangements they want. They reflect the understanding of a free society as not one large community but a community of communities. And like most forms of private regulation, they offer several advantages over state regulation: flexibility, small scale, voluntariness and a wide array of choices.

Rules of Etiquette

WELCOME TO THE SHOPS AT NATIONAL PLACE

In order to provide a safe, secure and pleasant shopping experience, we ask for your cooperation in complying with the rules of etiquette to be followed by all patrons. These activities are prohibited at The Shops at National Place:

1. Loitering
2. Smoking
3. Solicitation in The Shops
4. Presence in The Shops without shoes or shirt
5. Any act which could result in physical harm to persons or property
6. Use of loud or obscene language or gestures
7. Blocking store fronts, fire exits or stairways
8. Standing or walking in large groups which cause an inconvenience to others
9. Running, shouting, horseplay, throwing any type of object or debris, disorderly or disruptive conduct of any nature
10. The playing of radios or musical instruments unless part of an activity approved in advance by The Shops Management
11. Use of skateboards, roller skates or bicycles on The Shops property

---

12. Literature distribution without the written permission of The Shops Management
13. Possession of alcoholic beverages or illegal substances
14. Any criminal act under any federal, state or local statute or ordinance
15. Use of public restroom facility for any purpose other than intended (e.g., sinks for washing of face and hands only).

A violation of these rules may result in expulsion from The Shops or other legal action as deemed necessary.

Conclusion

REGULATION WITHOUT THE STATE IS ALL AROUND US. I'll mention just a few examples in closing. Companies such as Microsoft, Novell and Cisco Systems offer certification for people who pass examinations proving their skills in handling complex engineering tasks. These certification programmes are not only an important form of private regulation, they may well be the leading edge of an educational revolution in which businesses will look to such examinations and certificates rather than to diplomas and degrees of dubious quality when judging job applicants. Another part of the education revolution is the growing number of government, non-profit, and for-profit entities publishing data on schools to help parents make informed decisions.[11] I have on my desk the fourth edition of *Codes of Professional Responsibility,* a book of 1149 pages that includes codes of ethics for hundreds of business, medical, and legal associations.[12] The website *www.getnetwise.org* offers parents advice on regulating their children's use of the internet and links to more than 100 software tools for monitoring and regulating internet use. Instead of a one-size-fits-all government

---

[11] Doug Smith, 'One-Stop Research on Schools', *Los Angeles Times*, 20 October 1999, p. B2.

[12] Rena A. Gorlin, ed., *Codes of Professional Responsibility: Ethics Standards in Business, Health, and Law*, 4th ed., Washington, DC: Bureau of National Affairs, 1999.

censor, such competing forms of regulation allow individuals, families, and businesses to select the level and type of regulation that they prefer. The American Society for Testing and Materials coordinates 132 standards-writing committees and publishes standard test methods, specifications, practices, guides, classifications, and terminology. More than 10,000 ASTM standards are published each year in the 72 volumes of the *Annual Book of ASTM Standards*, used throughout the world.

Although private regulation surrounds us, there are many opportunities for expanding it. Yilmaz offers some suggestions, as does Regulation without the State. Other authors have suggested that the US government replace Food and Drug Administration regulation on medical devices with third-party certification[13] or that market arrangements replace subsidized crop insurance for American farmers.[14] Regulation without the state warrants both further research and wider use.

---

[13] Noel D. Campbell, 'Replace FDA Regulation of Medical Devices with Third-Party Certification', Washington, DC: Cato Institute, Policy Analysis no. 288, 12 November 1997.

[14] Jerry R. Skees, 'Agricultural Risk Management or Income Enhancement', *Regulation* 22 no. 1 (1999).

COMMENTARY:

OFHOTWATBOT:
A REGULATORY TALE[1]
Christopher Fildes

THE RISE AND DEMISE OF OFHOTWATBOT is a story with a moral for our regulated times. It shows what can happen when history takes a wrong turning and sets off down the road that is notoriously paved with good intentions – but it has a virtually happy ending.

Twenty years ago, when this story begins, the government of the day had just abolished exchange control and put 750 controllers in the Bank of England out of work. The Bank was at pains to look after them. It gave them generous terms, and even arranged for Warburgs to manage their money. This was the turning point.

In what passes for real life, the Bank somehow got the wrong Warburgs. The money was entrusted, not to the mighty house of S.G. Warburg and its eminent investment managers, but to Norton Warburg, no relation and not at all the same thing. Soon enough, 'Norty' Warburg had gone up in smoke and the money went with it.

Picture the red faces in the Bank. It had to pay up all over again, and the Governor developed a sudden interest in investor protection. There ought to be a law and a regulator, he thought. He pressed for them and got them, but today's government wants even more regulation, and has enacted a new law to give its regulators all the powers they could wish.

In virtual reality, though, the Bank got the right Warburgs – not difficult, surely. The money was safe, honour satisfied, and the Governor headed for his flat high above the City, proud but weary.

---

[1] OfHotWatBot was first narrated as a Hobart Lunch talk at the Institute of Economic Affairs on 29 October 1999 and reappeared in the *Daily Telegraph*'s City pages on 1 November.

He climbed straight into bed and stretched out his feet to the welcoming glow of his hot water bottle. It burst. Picture his furious face, his scalded toes, his waterlogged bed, his wakeful night on the sofa. He developed an immediate interest in pedal protection, and hopped back to the Bank to say so. A professor came up with an elaborate system of regulation, and his report found its way into law as the Footwarming Services Act, to be enforced by the Office of Hot Water Bottle Regulation, or OfHotWatBot.

Filling the office proved harder, but finally Sir Dedleigh Perrill was induced to take it on and went to work with zeal. He was a believer in scope, which meant that there was room for a rule about everything, and in polarisation, which meant that a hot water bottle, like the world, should be cold at its north and south poles but warm in the middle. This so obsessed him that he missed what happened when ministers launched a campaign, encouraging people to trade in their National Health Service bedsocks for personal hot water bottles, or hotties. Some did well by the swap but some holders of hotties were hotted, and the regulators looked the other way.

The truth only came out under his successors at OfWatHotBot, Sir David Chatter and Sir Andrew Largepileofpaperwork. They struggled to put matters right but by that time the trail, like the hotties, had gone cold. The salesmen who promoted them had long since found new ways to make a living, and are now selling thermal underwear over the internet. After the hotty affair, it took time and persistence to buy a hot water bottle at all. Buyers had to fill in questionnaires designed to establish (for the record) that they had been appropriately advised and knew how to boil a kettle. Retailers found it all too much and shut up shop. They, too, had to earn a living and many of them were re-trained as regulators, to make life harder for their surviving competitors. Regulation had become a growth industry, and retailing hot water bottles was not.

Even so, the pressure mounted for a yet more comprehensive scheme of regulation. All agreed that the existing law was badly drafted. What about the hazards of electric blankets? (Shocking.) What about warm bricks with towels wrapped round them? (Bruising.) What about dogs that tunnel their way into bed and curl up? (Barking.) There ought to be a law and, of course, compensation, too.

The trouble was that, as Professor Charles Goodhart observed, if regulation is perceived as a free benefit, people will always want more of it. In fact a free benefit is as unlikely in this life as a free lunch. More regulators mean more costs and more regulation means less choice. From that point of view the only thing worse than the first Footwarming Services Act was always going to be the next one.

At last there came a government prepared to put that proposition to the test. It set out to draft a new Act, which would be administered by a new and enlarged and empowered OfHotWatBot, under a new regulator-in-chief, Howard Youliketoloseyourlicence. Soon its new office at Budgerigar Dock housed 2,000 regulators and was bursting at the seams. Some of the powers assigned to OfHotWatBot were without precedent. They were said to make Magna Carta look minimal and to leave the Bill of Rights dishonoured. Still the legislation ground its way through Parliament and had actually reached the statute book when the Governor (a new one, by this time) sat up.

Hang on a moment, he said. Do we need a special law about hot water bottles? Doesn't the law cover them already? Don't I remember something called the Sale of Goods Act? Goods had to be of merchantable quality and fit and proper for their purpose, and the courts would uphold the principles of fair and honest dealing. Surely that was good enough? He sent round to the Bank's lawyers, Freshfields, and asked for advice. Quite right, said the man from Freshfields, or nearly right, anyway. There is a leading case on this very subject. In *Priest v. Last*, a hot water bottle had burst and it was held that the injured party had a remedy against the vendor. Yes, yes, people will say that hot water bottles must have a regime of their own, just as they say that financial services must have one, but the long-established law of the land could do the regulators' job for them.

At this moment the two of them saw the light. Then, looking eastwards, they saw a great shaft of light over Budgerigar Dock and a tornado of paper rising to the heavens. OfHotWatBot was dissolving into air like an enchanter's palace. Nothing remained of this great regulatory edifice – nothing, that is, but its 2,000 inhabitants, who had been put out of work and would expect generous terms. A folk memory stirred in the Governor's mind: Norty something? He pulled a favour in Whitehall and arranged for an uncontroversial one-clause bill to slip through Parliament. This stated that, for the avoidance of doubt, the law governing the sale of goods should be taken as applying to financial services.

So much for virtual reality. What passes for real life bears some resemblance to it, but is, of course, less probable and makes less sense. There must still be a way to take the right turning and to reach the happy ending.

COMMENTARY:

THE CHALLENGE TO STATE
REGULATION
Lord Haskins

THE DEVELOPMENT OF COMPETITIVE MARKET ECON-
OMIES, starting in the middle of the nineteenth century, has been
accompanied by a relentless increase in state intervention to
protect lenders and investors, workers and consumers from being
treated unjustly by the market.

The Tory Peer Lord Shaftesbury, first introduced regulations to
protect workers – in his case, children – from exploitation. At the
end of the nineteenth century the US government decided that
Rockefeller's dominance of the oil market was not in the public
interest and ordered him to divest. In the interests of public health,
regulations were introduced to control UK milk processing, also in
the nineteenth century.

The twentieth century has seen the growing power of consumer-
ism, exemplified by the steady increase in regulation to protect
shoppers and consumers from being exploited or endangered.
During the past half-century, concerns about the environment have
led to a dramatic increase in regulations in this area.

Ironically, the creation of a Free Trade area in Europe has had to
be accompanied by extensive regulation to harmonise trading rules
across the European Union, and also to outlaw unfair protectionist
actions by member states.

All of these trends have created a massive and complex set of
international, national, local and private regulations. Business complains that excessive regulations undermine enterprise and competitiveness, but those who seek protection through regulation
continue to demand more and more. Inevitably both sides over-
state their case. Although regulations can inhibit the market

unnecessarily, and thereby become counterproductive, the past 50 years' experience, which has seen the greatest increase in regulation, has also seen the most remarkable sustained economic growth in our history. Similarly, those who seek to find most solutions through regulation are continuously disappointed by its relative ineffectiveness – classically, in Soviet Russia.

As individuals, assuming we are healthy and financially secure, we tend to resent regulation as an intrusive restraint on our liberty and feel confident of our ability to handle risk without help from the state. But when things go wrong we are quick to attribute blame to the state and its officers for not offering us sufficient protection.

In a modern society, vulnerable groups – the young, the old, the sick, the poor – look to the state for extensive protection through regulation, and there is a constant argument between those on the left who feel that these groups receive inadequate protection from market abuse and ill-fortune, and those on the right who argue that there is too much state interference which does not necessarily provide solutions, and can engender an unhealthy culture of dependence on state support amongst those receiving it.

My Task Force devotes its energies to assessing the merits of both arguments on a case-by-case basis. In examining an issue such as the national minimum wage, we apply what we consider to be five principles to determine the relevance and effectiveness of the regulation: transparency, proportionality, accountability, targeting and consistency. Although we are not policy-makers, the application of these principles inevitably leads us to question the wisdom of policies.

Over the past two years we have identified many circumstances when it is inappropriate for the state to regulate:

- When, as in the case of beef on the bone, a regulation is disproportionate to the risk and unenforceable.

- When the economic cost of enforcing the regulation far exceeds any benefit arising – for example, compulsory parental leave could put a small company out of business.

- When people can perfectly well sort problems out for themselves – unpasteurised milk, properly licensed and labelled, should be no threat to a healthy adult.

- When the intervention might lead to unexpected and undesirable consequences. A complete ban on genetically modified food development might lead to a crisis in global food supplies in the future.

- A costly risk-proof rail safety system might result in rail fares having to rise so high that people would use their infinitely more dangerous motor cars instead.

- High regulatory restraints on adventure activities are probably reducing the opportunities for young people to engage in them, thereby denying them the benefits of character-building and learning to cope with risk.

- Regulations can also give people a false sense of security. If a person passes the state's test to be a 'fit person' for a sensitive occupation, such as child care or an adventure activity, that does not necessarily mean that all is well. The parent must retain the prime responsibility for the welfare of the child.

Regulations are, all too frequently, used by government in order to court short-term popularity or to be seen to be doing something in the face of a crisis. European Commissioners and European Members of Parliament have sought much-needed popularity by proposing well-intended regulations, such as the Working Time Directive, which are almost impossible to enforce consistently at local and national level. In the light of the Lyme Bay boating tragedy a few years ago, and a small number of awful attacks by wicked dogs, government ministers rushed to introduce regulations which have been confused, ineffective and counterproductive. The Dangerous Dog regulations had to be repealed, and we have, unsuccessfully so far, pressed the government to abandon the Adventure Licensing Scheme.

The Task Force is keen, where possible, to find solutions to problems without resorting to state regulation. Self-regulation, widely used by professional bodies and endorsed by government, has many attractions. The enforcers, being members of the profession, have the expertise needed to evaluate failures. The sense of professional pride and self-respect is a powerful motivator. Self-regulation is also bound to be cheaper than state intervention. Doctors, accountants, lawyers and chartered surveyors, all self regulate, albeit with varying levels of state endorsement, including legislation. Why not get teachers to regulate themselves, instead of relying entirely on Ofsted? It is much better for the Stock Exchange to regulate its members, rather than develop a costly bureaucratic state system.

However, there are valid concerns about shortcomings in self-regulation. The vested interest of mutual protection can take precedence over the public interest. The Task Force's principles seem to be as appropriate for 'self' as they are for 'state' regulation. The main concerns relate to secrecy, lack of accountability and inconsistency, and these can be tested against the principles.

Some self-regulatory regimes are not satisfactory, notably those affecting lawyers and house-builders and, because of that, those who self regulate should agree their procedures with government and should publish reports on their effectiveness. The handling of complaints is a critical aspect – these must be analysed, published, and action taken when unacceptable evidence is produced.

I strongly support the case for more self-regulation. Take, for example, food safety. It cannot be in the interests of a leading food retailer, or a food manufacturer's board or a high quality restaurant, to endanger the well-being of their customers through neglect and short-cutting. Therefore it is a waste of time and effort for the state's enforcers to regulate these groups extensively. Much better that the effort is put on helping smaller businesses who may lack the knowledge and expertise to comply with necessary safety standards.

However, for this approach to work, the public and the media must respond sensibly and proportionately when failures in self-regulation occur, as they inevitably will. There are 170,000 doctors in Britain, 100,000 working in the National Health Service. The fact that several hundred have been struck off the register should not surprise us – indeed, statistically, it should be reassuring, assuming that the system is succeeding in identifying all of those who do not meet the standards of performance and behaviour expected. But too often, one case, such as the Bristol babies tragedy, can lead to over-reaction from the media and the public calling for further state intervention, rather than looking at ways of improving the quality of existing self-regulation.

There is one professional group for which I feel that self-regulation is not the answer. Failures in policing can have such an impact on public confidence, as in the Lawrence case, as to undermine the effectiveness of law enforcement and the protection of the safety and liberty of citizens. The Police Complaints procedure, a mixture of self-regulation and non-transparent insider investigation, damages the credibility of the police in the minds of the public and should be replaced by a fully transparent investigatory process, independent of the police.

Most business people, large and small, grumble about the burdens of state regulation, but in fact the main problem lies with small businesses (SMEs). Indeed, larger companies can often use state regulation to obtain competitive advantage over smaller ones. For example, when the recent Food Standards Agency was being debated, many larger businesses wanted a strict licensing regime to apply to all food premises, recognising that the costs and time incurred by many smaller firms might even put them out of business. Fortunately, we prevailed on the government to reject this unfair and unenforceable approach.

Frequently, new regulations, especially in the employment area, have no impact on the larger, more progressive enterprises. Most were already paying well above the national minimum wage and offering unpaid parental leave to those who wanted it. One might conclude, therefore, that the main purpose of regulatory proposals is to bring small employers into line with the practices already established by their larger brethren. Undoubtedly, most of the worst abuses of employees and of customers are from the smaller firms who tend to be less well invested and to lack the knowledge, skills and resources needed to be good employers.

There are those who make the case for exempting small businesses from regulatory compliance, but as many regulations exist because of shortcomings in the small business sector it hardly makes sense to exempt them. If there is a case for a small business exemption, there is a case for withdrawing the regulation completely.

The danger of an under-regulated market is that two categories of employers will emerge. The larger, conscious of their public reputation, keen to attract the best people, offer excellent conditions to their staff, including generous pension schemes. The smaller, less affluent, have no such qualms about their reputation, and will be inclined to offer as minimal conditions as they can get away with. Reputable small businesses frequently support regulations which ensure that their more cynical competitors pay proper wages. Two further points need to be made.

- First, the larger employers are constantly reducing the number of people they employ, either through improved productivity or through outsourcing as much of their services as possible, thereby taking advantage of the less expensive small business labour market. Practically all the new jobs in a modern economy emanate from the small business sector.

- Secondly, the informal, cyclical nature of much of this work undoubtedly appeals to many people who do not seek full time employment, and prefer to move in and out of the labour market at will.

I do not believe that there are straightforward preferred options to this problem. The heavily regulated labour markets in Germany inhibit legitimate job creation, especially in the service industries, and contribute to the relatively high unemployment figures there. But in Germany there is a thriving grey economy, where many of these services are supplied outside the law. And the quality of legitimate employment is very high, as are the benefits available to the unemployed.

In the US, on the other hand, where small business labour markets are largely unregulated, jobs abound in the service areas and unemployment figures are much lower. But the quality of many of these jobs is poor, as are the social security safety nets, so levels of inequality and insecurity are relatively higher.

There does not appear to be a significant difference in economic performance because of these two approaches to labour market regulation. True, in the last few years, America has boomed whereas Germany has been static, but much of that can be attributed to the cost of unification and the acute employment problems in East Germany.

Over a longer period, Germany has grown slightly quicker than the US and is now set to outperform over the next few years. France, also heavily regulated, has performed similarly.

Britain, in the middle of the regulatory road, has done better than Germany in recent years, but this after many years of relative underperformance. The UK GDP per capita is still somewhat below that of France and West Germany, and well below that of the US. Much of this can be attributed to an inadequate educational system which has resulted in chronic skill shortages and a depressing surplus of unskilled workers in the market. Our regulatory regimes do not appear to be a significant factor in our low manufacturing competitiveness.

In the late nineteenth and early twentieth century, the state was keen to regulate to protect its citizens from moral hazard and from self-inflicted damage. We were told that we could not shop or enjoy ourselves on Sundays; we are still limited from buying a drink whenever a bar wants to sell us one; until the Lady Chatterley case in the 1960s, we had extensive censorship of books, films and the theatres. The Americans had a futile experiment with prohibition, and most countries, equally futilely, ban cannabis but not tobacco. In principle, the state should seek to repeal all regulations aimed at protecting citizens from themselves, except for the protection of children, though these restrictions are easily overcome by today's resourceful youths. However, although most people recognise the inadequacy of regulation in these areas, the political sensitivities prevent any extensive deregulation.

Insurance can be an effective alternative to state regulation. Indeed, Lloyd George and Beveridge planned to fund the Welfare State through National Insurance, and today's German social security is still effectively funded out of personal and corporate insurance contributions. Its great advantage over funding out of general taxation is that it gives recipients a sense of ownership, and promotes mutuality. One would expect more participation, less abuse of the system, and consequently less regulation. Unfortunately, the principle of insurance has been gradually eroded in Britain's social security system, in favour of funding out of general taxation, resulting in less commitment and more abuses.

Insurance can also be a more effective protection for consumers than state intervention. The Association of British Travel Agents protects people's holidays when one of their members goes into liquidation. Trade unions increasingly offer their members legal support when their rights are jeopardised. Other forms of mutual co-operation, which offer support and protection without the state intervening, include trade associations, the churches, company pension and sickness schemes, and most voluntary agencies.

A more educated, more prosperous society should, on the face of it, require less protection from the state than a poor illiterate one. Yet it appears that the more informed, the more prosperous we are, the more regulation we seek. In the face of powerful consumer pressure groups, governments find it difficult to resist this trend. But it must be right, as much as possible, to expect well-informed citizens to work at their own solutions, rather than expecting state intervention on their behalf.

This is made more difficult because the public does not trust the government to give them balanced, sensible advice on how to deal with issues – a legacy of the BSE crisis. But it is right to persevere in rebuilding the public's confidence in the government's advice.

We should recognise that as parents and as employers, we have the prime responsibility for protecting the interests of our children, our old people and our staff. The state's regulatory system should be a fallback, a safety net for vulnerable groups, and should not allow parents and employers to abrogate their responsibilities.

Regulations to minimise risk create the greatest difficulties for the state. When accidents occur, the state and its agents are inevitably the first to be blamed. Small wonder that the temptation is for over-regulation and for risk-averse policy makers to seek risk-free solutions. Remarkable progress has been made in improving, for example, public transport safety. Aeroplanes are far safer because of radical engineering improvements and better staff training. The roads are far safer because of design improvements, better-constructed motor cars, extensive state regulation and propaganda to improve the performance of drivers. For the same reasons, workplaces are far safer than they were.

Yet public perceptions do not reflect these enormous improvements, rather the reverse. Most people think that their lives, and especially their children's lives, are more at risk than before. The media does not help – the exaggerated reporting of accidents and potential threats, often based on superficial, unscientific, anecdotal evidence, seems to sell newspapers and alarm the readers. False reassurances by governments in the past, particularly with regard to the nuclear industry and food, do not help, even though nuclear energy remains the safest of all, and British food is probably the safest in the world.

Persuading people to take a more balanced view about risks and to do more themselves in order to mitigate risk, will be a long job, as was the drink-drive campaign which took 20 years of relentless propaganda before becoming effective.

It is also necessary to get the public to be more rational, more tolerant of regulatory failure, assuming those responsible have done their best in the circumstances. Otherwise, people in the public sector who are paid to take risks, such as social workers, will choose options which are less likely to expose them to public criticism, but may well be the most risky in the long term. It is almost always best to leave a child with its parents, however risky the circumstances, rather than take it into institutionalised care. But, by taking the child into care, the social worker will be less exposed to criticism if things go wrong.

It seems ironic that a society which has a low regard for the state and its officers, which, through affluence and education, should have less need for protection provided by the state, and which is reluctant to pay taxes, nevertheless demands more and more intervention from the state. It is also true that this last half-century has seen far more state intervention – a huge increase in the state's control over GDP – but also a remarkable growth in general prosperity, with the standard of living rising three- or fourfold.

Nevertheless, the need to challenge intervention, and to ensure that when interventions are necessary they are fair and effective, is essential if such prosperity is to be maintained and enhanced.

COMMENTARY:

THE ROLE OF PRIVATE REGULATION IN MAINTAINING GLOBAL FINANCIAL STABILITY

Randall S. Kroszner

MANY INTERNATIONAL FINANCIAL TRANSACTIONS occur in a realm that is close to anarchy. Although numerous committees and organisations attempt to coordinate domestic regulatory policies and negotiate international standards, they have no enforcement powers. The Cayman Islands and Bermuda offer not only beautiful beaches but also harbours safe from most financial regulation and international agreements. When contractual disputes arise in international financial transactions, it is often highly uncertain where they would be litigated and what laws would apply.

Yet, international financial markets and institutions have grown rapidly and have performed remarkably well. The unregulated Euro market, where securities issuers go to avoid domestic securities regulation, for example, has grown from nothing 30 years ago to a multi-trillion dollar market without a major incident. In fact, the growth of many of the largest and most active international financial markets has been spurred by the avoidance of traditional government regulation. Frauds, mismanagement, and bankruptcies do occur – sometimes on a spectacular scale, as the collapse of BCCI and Barings illustrate – but market forces have been effective regulators that have created order out of the apparent chaos of the international banking and financial markets.

The overall stability and integrity of these markets is due primarily to the role of private regulators, not public ones. To be successful in this anarchic but orderly realm, firms and markets must develop strategies that promote credibility and induce contractual performance, largely without recourse to traditional government-supplied legal devices. Striving for competitive advantage in these markets tends to generate the private regulation that then accounts for the success of international financial markets. This process well illustrates how effective 'regulation without the state'[1] can and does emerge. My emphasis in this brief commentary is on how innovations in strategic organisational design and governance for financial institutions can handle international regulatory challenges more effectively than traditional public regulation.

Private Strategic Responses

THE PRIVATE STRATEGIC RESPONSES to concerns about stability and integrity take many forms. A traditional solution had been to create a members-only club, with high standards for membership. Clearing houses and organised exchanges are the classic examples of this approach. Long before regulators were setting minimum capital and liquidity standards, bankers were policing each others' private note issuance through privately developed clearing systems during the so-called free banking eras in eighteenth and nineteenth century Scotland, and through the Suffolk System in New England early nineteenth century US.[2] Since the nineteenth century, the clearing house associations of the Chicago Board of Trade and Chicago Mercantile Exchanges have been monitoring the financial health of their members and provide a form of insurance against failure of the clearing members.[3]

Most recent growth in the international markets, however, has been taking place outside traditional members-only institutions.

---

[1] John Blundell and Colin Robinson, *Regulation Without the State*, London: Institute of Economic Affairs, Occasional Paper 109, 1999.

[2] Randall Kroszner, 'Are Self-Regulated Payments Systems Efficient? A Comment on Calomiris and Kahn', *Journal of Money, Credit, and Banking*, 2 (November 1996), pp. 798–803; Randall S. Kroszner, 'Free Banking: Lessons from the Scottish Experience for Emerging Market Economies', Chapter 3 in Gerard Caprio, ed., *Reforming Finance: Historical Implications for Policy*, New York: Cambridge University Press, 1997; Charles Calomiris, and Charles Kahn, 'The Efficiency of a Self-Regulated Payments System: Learning from the Suffolk System', *Journal of Money, Credit, and Banking*, 2 (November 1996), pp. 766–797.

[3] Randall S. Kroszner, 'Can the Financial Markets Privately Regulate Risk? The Development of Derivatives Clearinghouses and Recent Over-the-Counter Innovations', *Journal of Money, Credit, and Banking*, 2 (August 1999), pp. 596–618.

Over-the-counter (OTC) derivatives trading, for example, has grown sharply during the last decade and, since 1994, has exploded. Much of the movement toward OTC markets is driven by the desire to avoid the domestic regulation that has been imposed over time on organised exchanges. Since OTC markets have no physical location, sovereign regulators have much difficulty in claiming that such activity falls within their jurisdictions.

In these effectively unregulated OTC markets, the strategic responses to the challenges of stability and integrity have taken a variety of forms. Independent credit-rating agencies play a key role in certifying the quality of potential counter-parties to a transaction. These third-party monitors publicly grade the health of the major players. Contracts that involve long-term relationships often include clauses that permit early termination if a counter-party falls below a specified rating threshold. Some participants simply will not deal with others that do not meet a minimum rating. Private regulators have thus fulfilled the auditing, screening and monitoring functions of the public regulators and have been quite effective even though they do not have the same legal powers to obtain information that public regulators do.

The emphasis on top ratings is a market-generated response to concerns about the risks of entering long-term contracts in the OTC derivative market. As many institutions saw their ratings slip by the early 1990s, they began to face increasing costs of participating in these markets and were excluded entirely from some transactions. These firms then made the strategic decision to create new organisational forms to address the concerns about credit risk.

The innovation is a special purpose vehicle, called a derivative product company (DPC), that would be structured to garner a top rating. Less than high-grade institutions incorporated DPC subsidiaries which have capital and governance structure distinct from the parent. A DPC can win a triple-A rating because its capital cannot be tapped by creditors of the parent company if the parent becomes bankrupt. Also, it may have a credit enhancements that do not rely upon the health of the parent. Moody's and Standard and Poor's provide flexible definitions of DPC structure to allow firms to achieve triple-A status in a variety of ways. This strategic restructuring of the firm thereby improved the long-term

71

stability and integrity of these derivative markets and the innovation was driven by market forces.

In addition to the rapid growth in derivatives, cross-border lending and international securities issues are at record highs. The role of banks in these activities raises another challenge for stability and integrity in the international markets; namely, the conflict of interest that can arise when underwriting and lending are combined. Consider a firm that suddenly experiences a shock that is likely to reduce its future profitability. A bank with a lending relationship to that firm may know before the market does that the firm's prospects have now dimmed. The bank's superior knowledge, however, is a double-edged sword. If the bank were free from conflicts, the bank would make an objective analysis of the firm's future and, if new securities were to be issued, reveal the information to the public. Alternatively, a rogue bank may try to take advantage of its superior knowledge by underwriting and distributing securities to an unsuspecting public and using the proceeds to repay the outstanding bank loan.

This concern was a key factor driving the passage of the 1933 Glass–Steagall Act in the US which forbids commercial banks from underwriting and dealing in corporate securities.[4] The fear that such conflicts can then lead to a destabilising loss of confidence in public securities markets continues to be a major obstacle to permitting universal banking in the US and plays an important role in the debate over financial reform in transition and emerging economies. The public regulatory solution generally involves mandating complete separation or strict 'Chinese walls' between lending and underwriting operations.

Market forces, however, have been able to provide the incentives for banks to reduce the potential for conflicts voluntarily through the strategic reorganisation of the firm. Banks that lack credibility are penalised in the marketplace because purchasers will pay lower

---

[4] Randall S. Kroszner, 'The Evolution of Universal Banking and Its Regulation in Twentieth Century America', in Anthony Saunders and Ingo Walter, eds., *Universal Banking: Financial System Design Reconsidered*, New York: Irwin Professional Publishers, 1996; Randall S. Kroszner and Raghuram G. Rajan, 'Is the Glass–Steagall Act Justified? A Study of the US Experience with Universal Banking before 1933', *American Economic Review*, 84 (September 1994), pp. 810–832.

prices and demand higher yields from securities underwritten by institutions they cannot trust. Prior to the Glass–Steagall Act in the US, banks organised their investment banking operations either as an internal securities department within the bank or as a separately incorporated and capitalised affiliate with its own board of directors.

In a study with Raghuram Rajan,[5] we found that the internal departments obtained lower prices than did the separate affiliates for otherwise similar issues they underwrote. The pricing penalty associated with the internal department is consistent with investors' discounting for the greater likelihood of conflicts problems when lending and underwriting are done within the same structure. We found that the pricing benefit for the separate affiliates increased with the number of affiliate board members who were independent of the parent bank. Banks thus can enhance their underwriting credibility and performance through a strategic reorganisation which separates the lending and underwriting and uses independent board members as internal monitors. Consequently, we also found that US banks increasingly adopted the separate affiliate structure in the decade prior to the passage of the Glass–Steagall Act.

German universal banks, which had traditionally underwritten through internal departments, have now been moving these operations out to separate affiliates in London. Until recently, the German securities markets had been relatively uncompetitive and dominated by the banks themselves, with relatively low participation by individuals or outsiders. In these circumstances, the major players would be equally well-informed so there would be little value in setting up a separate structure. To achieve credibility in an internationally competitive market, however, they have found it in their interest to separate these functions. Market competition thus propels banks voluntarily to adopt Chinese wall structures without any regulatory requirements.[6]

---

[5] Randall Kroszner and Raghuram Rajan, 'Organization Structure and Credibility: Evidence from Commercial Bank Securities Activities before the Glass–Steagall Act', *Journal of Monetary Economics,* 39 (August 1997), pp. 475–516.

[6] Randall S. Kroszner, Testimony before the Committee on Banking and Financial Services, US House of Representatives, 29 April 1998.

Public Regulatory Responses

HAVING EXAMINED THE PRIVATE STRATEGIC RESPONSES to promote stability and integrity in the anarchy of the international markets, let us now consider the roles and incentives of public regulators. Public regulators can and often do perform the same functions as the credit rating agencies by evaluating and rating the soundness of financial institutions. The incentives of the private and public regulators are quite different. The private rating agencies are rewarded for being the most effective and accurate monitor, particularly for being the first to spot a problem and warn the public about it. In contrast, distress that would trigger a downgrade is perceived as trouble not only for the institution but for the regulators as well. No one holds S&P responsible when a firm experiences a shock that lowers its credit quality.

To avoid taking the blame, public regulators have an incentive to delay recognising and publicly announcing problems, since there is a chance that a positive shock could eventually resolve the distress, and waiting could allow them to put burden on future regulators or politicians. The poor record of US regulators during the 1980s, giving high grades to institutions whose failures were imminent, and the consistently extreme official underreporting of the bad loan problem in Japan during the 1990s illustrate this tendency. In the US Savings and Loan crisis, for example, the desire to put off the day of reckoning led regulators to undertake perverse policies that obscured problems in the short run – such as permitting economically insolvent institutions to pay dividends – but were extremely costly to taxpayers in the long run.[7]

In addition, public regulators cannot be insulated from political and interest group pressures. In Chicago, the police cars are emblazoned with the phrase 'we serve and protect', and often that phrase can be applied to public regulators. Rather than promote the public interest, the regulators may end up serving the private interest of the industry that they are regulating and protect it from

---

[7] Randall Kroszner and Philip Strahan, 'Regulatory Incentives and the Thrift Crisis: Dividends, Mutual-to-Stock Conversions, and Financial Distress', *Journal of Finance*, 51 (September 1996), pp. 1285–1320.

competition.[8] The political pressures provide a background incentive different than for the private regulators.

Finally, the public regulators have much greater difficulty accommodating the dynamic change of the market than do the private regulators. Moody's and S&P can provide general guidelines for good practice and then exercise their judgement as innovations occur through time. Giving public regulators wide discretion is an invitation to political and interest group pressure.

Conclusions for Regulatory Reform

THE KEY LESSON FOR REGULATORY REFORM is that public regulation should not be permitted to crowd out dynamic private regulation. Strategic organisational choices by financial institutions and third-party monitors such as credit rating agencies have been quite successful in providing stability and integrity for the international financial markets. Although the market is not a perfect regulator – for instance the Caymans can provide a haven for rogues – the public regulatory alternative should not interfere with the creative experimentation and innovation that the lovely beaches of the Caymans foster.

One of the proposals from the 1999 G-7 summit in Denver was to increase information sharing and coordination among the public regulators. If that information is also shared with the public, applying the regulators' advice to the markets for greater transparency to themselves, then this effort is to be applauded. Some, such as Henry Kaufmann, have gone further to suggest that an international super-regulator be created to set common standards worldwide. A unified international regulator is likely to slow the engine that generates the innovations that have driven the spectacular growth of the international financial markets without any clear stability advantages.

To ensure that public regulation is effective at promoting stability, such regulations should be subject to a rough cost–benefit analysis. A number of distinguished regulatory experts in different fields have recommended that such a common-sense test be applied in health,

---

[8] George Stigler, ed., *Chicago Studies in Political Economy*, Chicago: University of Chicago Press, 1988.

safety, and the environment.[9] Although certainly the quantification of the costly and benefits of many financial regulations is extremely difficult, the challenges would appear to be no greater in environment and safety areas where decisions are made about infrequent but highly costs events, much like financial crises. Emphasis on the costs and benefits of such regulation would greatly clarify the public debate and undoubtedly improve the nature of financial regulation.

---

[9] Robert Hahn and Robert Litan, *Improving Regulatory Accountability*, Washington, DC: American Enterprise Institute and Brookings Institution, 1997.

COMMENTARY:
THE DEVIL OR THE DEEP BLUE SEA?
Graeme Leach

The Intervention Index

THIS PAPER AIMS TO SHOW THAT when Government intervention in the economy is looked at in its entirety a very worrying picture emerges. The Intervention Index – public spending and regulation as a proportion of GDP – is deteriorating under New Labour and is surely at alarming levels in the rest of the EU. Government intervention has evolved into the current situation of the devil or the deep blue sea – more spending and/or more regulation?

A recent European Policy Forum paper[1] has stated:

> The extent of Government intervention in the economy is usually measured by relating public expenditure or the tax burden to GDP. The allocative costs of mandatory regulations … appear neither in national statistics nor in Government budgets. This means that the true degree of Government intervention is underestimated and its negative implications for static and dynamic efficiency underrated.

Government has a choice in deciding how to intervene in economic life or whether to intervene at all. For example, it can decide to target low income earners with additional income support (thereby increasing public expenditure) or by legislating for a minimum wage (thereby increasing intervention without increasing expenditure). The concern over 'stealth' interventionism is most apparent at the EU level where the European Commission's budget is restricted to 1.27% of pan-EU GDP.

Concern over the regulatory threat from the EU is further highlighted by public choice theory which shows how regulation

---

[1] P. Stein, T. D. Hopkins and R. Vaubel, *The Hidden Costs of Regulation in Europe,* London: European Policy Forum, September 1995.

benefits well organised interest groups. It is estimated that 72% of the EU budget and at least 78% of EU legislation is devoted to interest groups.[2] Andersen and Eliassen[3] have argued that:

> the EC system is now more lobbying-orientated than any national European system.

Regulatory rhetoric and reality

ALL TOO OFTEN THE CONCERN over the regulatory burden as expressed in political rhetoric is a world apart from the reality. In the US, during the Reagan Presidency, the regulatory burden did subside (see below). However, despite Vice-President Quayle's chairing of a deregulation task force the regulatory burden subsequently increased during the Bush administration. Vice-President Al Gore's 'Re-inventing Government' initiative has also failed to stem the upward tide in regulation during the Clinton administration.

The total regulatory cost – paperwork, price and entry controls, environmental and risk reduction – per household in the US fell from just over $7,000 at the beginning of the 1980s to $5,200 at the end of the 1980s.[4] Thereafter it rose to just over $6,000 in the mid 1990s. In aggregate the total regulatory cost equated to $525 billion dollars – around 8% of GDP – in 1980, $490 billion in 1989, $600 billion in 1995 and a projected $660 billion in 2000. In other words, compliance costs amount to around half of total federal receipts. This two-to-one ratio suggests regulation in the US – and the UK – should be placed far higher up the political agenda.

In the UK the 'all talk and no action' charge can also be levelled. The Conservative Government established a system of compliance cost assessment (CCA) in 1986. In 1993 the President of the Board of Trade, Michael Heseltine, launched the Deregulation Initiative. A Deregulation Unit employing 43 civil servants was established. By 1997 around 1,000 regulations had been either simplified or

---

[2] R. Vaubel, 'The Public Choice Analysis of European Integration', *European Journal of Political Economy*, 10, 1994.

[3] B. Andersen and F. Eliassen, 'European Community Lobbying', *European Journal of Political Research*, 20, 1991.

[4] See T.D. Hopkins, *Federal Regulatory Burdens – An Overview*, London: European Policy Forum, 1995.

scrapped, but the total estimated saving to business has been estimated at just £59 million.[5] In relation to the overall impact of
regulation this amount is mere pennies.

SMEs not only face the ongoing costs of implementing
regulatory requirements, but it often takes up substantial resources
and management time to understand the legislation in the first
place. Valuable time and money that could be better spent elsewhere. A 1997 survey by the Institute of Directors (IoD)[6] found
that 80% of companies needed to seek external advice concerning
regulatory requirements, and of these, 70% needed to hire private
consultants. Unsurprisingly, half the companies surveyed found
regulatory requirements to be time consuming and costly.

The New Labour government has increased regulation as a
central plank of policy. Press reports state that in 1999 there was a
regulatory avalanche in the UK with 3,438 issued by the Government – a new record.[7]

In combination with the rising tax share,[8] the raft of expensive
regulatory measures has produced a very damaging 'double
whammy' on economic incentives. Since coming to power New
Labour has instigated the national minimum wage, working time
regulations, increases in unfair dismissal compensation limits, parental leave regulations, European works councils, working families
tax credit and the new stakeholder pension. The IoD estimates –
using official government figures – that the combined compliance
cost of these regulations will be over £5 billion per annum.[9]

Commenting on such developments, Bill Jamieson, the former
economics editor of the *Sunday Telegraph* has written that such
measures display:

> a neurotic spasm of fiddling measures, born of a belief that it is
> Governments not markets that make us entrepreneurial, that

---

[5] Alison Cansfield, *Deregulation, Economic Comment*, London: Institute of Directors,
January 1997.

[6] Natasha Howard, *Better Regulation*, London: Institute of Directors, November 1997.

[7] 'Blair's Red Tape Record', *Sunday Telegraph*, 16 January 2000.

[8] R. Baron and G. Leach, *Budget 2000: Take No Chances*, London: Institute of Directors,
January 2000.

[9] 'Reg Alert', London: Institute of Directors, *Regulation Comment*, July 1999.

regulation not self-interest make us good corporate citizens, that tax fiddling not the removal of tax makes for enterprise.[10]

Turning a blind eye

THE NEW LABOUR GOVERNMENT has extended CCAs to regulatory impact assessments (RIA) but it is difficult to believe that there is any real intent to reduce the regulatory burden. The Regulatory Impact Unit (RIU) has also produced a guide to better European regulation. But where's the beef? The RIU is unable to provide any estimate of the aggregate cost of regulation. In fact the clearly stated aim of government policy is that it doesn't want to find out.

When asked for an estimate of the aggregate impact of regulatory measures the RIU responded to the IoD with a facsimile of two parliamentary questions when the Minister for the Cabinet Office was asked what estimate the Government have made of the cumulative impact on British business of changes in the degree and level of regulation since 1 May 1997. The Minister responded that:

> the type and incidence of the burden imposed by each regulation can be quite different and the costs cannot be added together ... the Government do not therefore publish cumulative figures.

In a separate question the Minister for the Cabinet Office was asked if the Government would publish the total costs of compliance with statutory regulations to all UK businesses and also those with less than 100 employees. The Minister responded:

> No. The Government do not, and do not intend, to publish estimates in the form requested.

This failing in public policy is alarming. The government has no firm estimates of the impact of its own regulatory legislation let alone the additional burden imposed by directives from the EU. The government is ignoring a critical opportunity and requirement for 'joined-up government'. There is of course method in this madness. How can political opposition be rallied against a hidden

---

[10] 'How to Bury Business Alive', *Sunday Telegraph*, 14 November 1999.

enemy? If there is no attempt to measure regulation, how can there be any attempt to control it?

When estimating the economic impact of regulations three sets of costs need to be considered:

- the direct administrative and compliance costs incurred by the private sector

- the labour and capital costs incurred by the public sector regulatory bodies

- the indirect costs incurred by private sector companies and consumers as a result of the implementation of regulations.

Estimates of these various costs are often difficult to produce, but as the analysis below shows, even partial availability of data supports the view that regulation has an enormous economic cost.

Just how big a problem is regulation?

A RECENT SURVEY BY THE IoD shows the regulatory burden to be stifling.[11] The survey found that 44% of companies cited the regulatory burden as a barrier to growth. Regulation was second to a lack of skilled labour (46%) and well ahead of other categories such as late payment (29%), access to finance (20%), unfair competition (20%) and the uniform business rate (15%).

In other words, at a time when the claimant unemployment count is a mere 4% and skill shortages are to be expected, the regulatory burden on companies is just as much a problem. The Prime Minister's political mantra is 'education, education, education'. One wonders whether it should be 'deregulation, deregulation, deregulation' instead.

The IoD survey found that of those citing regulation as a barrier to growth the most damaging regulatory areas were general Government policy (34%), employment and personnel regulations (17%) and the working time directive (12%).

In 1995 the Institute of Directors produced an assessment[12] of the costs of regulation based on Government compliance cost

---

[11] *Business Opinion Survey*, December 1999.

[12] *To Be Governed*, London: Institute of Directors, Papers on Deregulation, 1995.

assessments for individual regulations which were then grossed up for the whole economy. Our estimate, based on 48 CCAs in *The Management Information for Regulatory Reform* (which contained 7,000 pieces of regulation) was of an aggregate compliance cost of regulation of £43 billion. In 2000 prices that is roughly £50 billion per annum. The study found that in the case of just 25 pieces of legislation proposed by the Department of Social Security, the Department of Employment and the Department of the Environment the compliance burden alone was in excess of £2.5 billion.

The following analysis reviews a number of studies which have aimed to quantify the impact of regulation in the US, EU and UK. The studies focus on both the direct and indirect costs associated with regulation.

Peter Stein provides a useful overview of the international literature on the aggregate impact of regulation:

> The studies demonstrate persuasively that contrary to popular as-sumptions these direct costs are very big indeed ranging from an annual cost of one to four percent of GDP. When indirect costs are added the combined total of indirect and direct costs together rise to 8–9% of GDP. These figures pertain to the US from where most data exist. We know however that most, if not all European countries are more heavily regulated. It is therefore likely that similar studies on Europe would reveal figures at the top end of the range or of even greater magnitude.[13]

A 1995 report by the European Observatory for SMEs[14] esti-mated that the direct costs of national administrative regulatory burdens together with mandatory EU policy amounted to between 3–4% of GDP.

Professor Murray Weidenbaum has estimated that for the US every dollar spent on regulatory agencies resulted in a $20 cost increase for the private sector – attributable to extra administrative and compliance costs.

---

[13] *Measuring the Costs of Regulation*, London: European Policy Forum, 1995.

[14] *The European Observatory for SMEs*. Third Annual Report, EIM, The Netherlands, 1995.

Regulation does not just involve additional expenditure for the private sector, it clearly involves extra governmental activity as well – the taxpayer cost of public sector labour and capital operating the regulatory regime. The Centre for the Study of American Business (CSAB) has estimated that between 1970 and 1995 (constant prices) spending for economic regulation in the US more than doubled. CSAB estimate that spending for social regulation tripled over the same period.

In the UK, Sandford has estimated that the aggregate administrative and compliance costs of taxation amount to around 1.5% of GDP.[15] Significantly also, the Sandford study highlights the variation in regulatory impact across companies of different size – the smaller the business the greater the proportionate burden.

Available evidence strongly suggests that the regulatory burden falls most severely on SMEs. A European Commission report gives further evidence of the disproportionate impact on SMEs.[16] This report estimates that (in 1993 prices) the average cost of the administrative burden was 1,800 ECU per employee for all enterprises, but it amounted to 3,500 ECU per employee in enterprises with 1–9 employees but only 600 ECU per employee for those with more than 100 employees.

Most of the research on the indirect costs – lower prices and welfare gains to consumers – associated with regulation has been undertaken in the US. A recent notable study attempted to develop an empirical methodology to predict the impact of deregulation.[17] The US study suggested that the gains from deregulation, when translated over the whole economy, could amount to 7–9% of GDP.

Conclusion

TAKING THE US AS AN EXAMPLE, the direct and indirect costs of regulation could be huge, amounting to 9% of GDP in the UK. The studies cited above strongly suggest that the combined impact

[15] C. Sandford, *Administrative and Compliance Costs of Taxation*, Bath: Centre for Fiscal Studies, 1989.

[16] *The Group of Independent Experts on Legislative and Administrative Simplifications*, European Commission, 1995.

[17] C. Winston, 'Economic Deregulation: Days of Reckoning for Microeconomists', *Journal of Economic Literature*, September 1993.

of public spending and regulation – the Intervention Index – is rapidly approaching 50% of GDP under New Labour. In continental Europe the figure is likely to be well in excess of 60% of GDP.

Moreover, the EU Intervention Index is likely to rise much further in the future as a result of unfunded pension obligations and the extension of labour market and product regulation. Governments would do well to absorb the conclusions of the OECD that:

> Where there has been effective deregulation there have been efficiency gains. Almost all evidence concerning deregulation supports this view.[18]

---

[18] B. Molitor, *Regulatory Reform: Some Approaches from a European Perspective*, Paris: OECD, 1996.

COMMENTARY:

MARKET-BASED REGULATORY MECHANISMS
Yesim Yilmaz

Regulation Without the State provides a strong argument for the need to understand voluntary and market-based alternatives to government regulation. This need is particularly pressing with quality and safety regulations. Regulations governing quality and safety, together with environmental protection regulations are the fastest growing forms of government intervention.[1] At the same time, recent studies show that quality and safety regulations typically impose large costs on businesses and consumers without delivering comparable benefits.[2] Therefore, a critical examination of the rationale behind the state's involvement in quality and safety, and an evaluation of alternatives is timely.

Is there a case for quality and safety regulation by the state?

THE CASE FOR THE STATE'S INVOLVEMENT in quality and safety regulations is based on two premises.

---

[1] For further details, see Thomas D. Hopkins, *Regulatory Costs in Profile*, Center for the Study of American Business, Policy Paper No. 132, August 1996; and Melinda Warren and Murray Weidenbaum, *The Rise of Regulation Continues: An Analysis of the Budget for the Year 2000*, Center for the Study of American Business, Regulatory Budget Report 22, August 1999.

[2] Two recent reports from the US estimate that more than half the social regulations issued between 1982 and mid-1996 fail a cost-benefit test. These reports also note that eliminating those regulations would have increased the size of the economy by almost $300 billion. For details see Robert W. Crandall, Christopher DeMuth, Robert W. Hahn, Robert E. Litan, Pietro S. Nivola and Paul R. Portney, *An Agenda for Federal Regulatory Reform*, Washington DC: American Enterprise Institute and the Brookings Institution, 1997, and Robert W. Hahn and Robert E. Litan, *Improving Regulatory Accountability*, Washington DC: American Enterprise Institute and the Brookings Institution, 1997.

- First, the argument for state intervention assumes that markets typically fail to produce adequate information about product quality and safety.

- Second, the need for state intervention implies that in the absence of quality or safety information, deception by firms will inevitably crowd out good conduct. Since most quality attributes are not verifiable at the time of the purchase, in the absence of adequate information about quality, sellers would deceive their customers by offering dubious, shoddy, dangerous, or ineffective products. Therefore, the state is expected to step in and offer 'protection', typically in the form of product bans, minimum quality standards, and licensing.

However, a closer look at the markets refutes both of these premises.

- First of all, in developed economies, many private, independent institutions provide quality and safety information in an organised way. These institutions set standards, develop guidelines, extend certifications and ratings, perform inspections, issue reviews, and act as intermediaries between buyers and sellers. In these ways, market-based institutions perform functions akin to what is expected of government regulation: they help consumers make informed decisions, and ensure that businesses deliver what they promise.

- Second, even in the absence of detailed information, good conduct seems to be the norm, and not the exception. Advocates of state regulations typically promulgate consumers as the sole 'victims' of inadequate quality and safety information. In fact, if consumers cannot tell high quality products from low quality ones, firms committed to quality and safety also lose, because they cannot capture returns from high quality production.[3] Therefore, these firms have an incentive to establish credibility and differentiate themselves from

---

[3] The problem of 'bads' driving out the 'goods' is known as 'adverse selection' in the economics literature. See George A. Akerlof, 'The Market for "Lemons": Quality, Uncertainty, And Market Mechanism,' *Quarterly Journal of Economics* Vol. 84, 1970, pp. 488–500.

"fly-by-nights." Firms value their reputation, strive to build a long-term relation with their customers, and generally share the risks of possible quality defects by offering warranties.[4] These practices, when supplemented by a sound legal system, offer customers protection from unsafe and unhealthy products.

Market-based institutions that provide safety and quality information are common

REGULATION WITHOUT THE STATE presents some examples of market-based institutions that monitor products and services for quality and safety.[5] In fact, examples are plenty; even a brief glance at common household items, or frequently utilized services testifies to the market's success in sorting the quality from the dubious, and safe from the unsafe. Table 1 presents some other examples from the US.[6]

In the US, almost all electronic devices carry approval stamps from Underwriters' Laboratories. Food and other products with organic ingredients display approvals from kosher certifiers or organic certifiers. The American Dental Association monitors dental products for effectiveness; The American Heart Association endorses 'heart friendly' foods. Even the Internet, which has become a major source of product and service information, is monitored for the truthfulness and appropriateness of its contents. Referral agencies such as 1-800-DOCTORS provide information about health services, insurance rating companies inform customers about the solvency of insurance firms. By providing information to the potential creditors, personal credit agencies not only enable individuals to have easy access to credit markets, but also provide

---

[4] On reputation, see various essays in Daniel B. Klein, *Reputation: Studies in the Voluntary Elicitation of Good Conduct*, Ann Arbor: The University of Michigan Press, 1997; Benjamin Klein and Keith. B. Leffler, 'The Role of Market Forces in Assuring Contractual Performance.' *Journal of Political Economy*, Vol. 84, 1981, pp. 485–503. On warranties see Esther Gal-Or, 'Warranties as a Signal of Quality,' *Canadian Journal of Economics*, Vol. 22, No. 1, 1989, pp. 50–61

[5] *Regulation Without the State*, pp. 30–41 (pp. 18–19 of this Readings).

[6] For further details on how some of these organisations operate, see Yesim Yilmaz, 'Private Regulation: A Real Alternative for Regulatory Reform,' *Policy Analysis* 303, Cato Institute, Washington DC, April 1998.

Table 1: Examples of market-based information providers from the US

Organisation	What does it do?	How does it do it?
American Dental Association	Ensure that dental products are safe and effective, and advertisements are truthful	Standard Setting, certification, monitoring
Kosher certifiers such as Orthodox Union	Check for compliance with religious rules	Certification and monitoring
Organic food certifiers such as Oregon Tilth	Check for 'organic' qualities in ingred-ients	Standard Setting, certification and monitoring
TV Ratings	Inform advertisers about the value of the advertising medium such as airtime, and recently the Internet	Rating and monitoring
Internet content ratings	Inform web-users about the quality of the contents	Rating and monitoring
Financial ratings	Inform investors about the solvency of debt and equity issuers	Rating and monitoring
Personal credit ratings	Inform creditors about the credit risk associated with borrowers	Reviews
Reference services	Inform customers about the quality of various services	Reviews
Insurance ratings	Inform customers about the solvency of insurance companies	Rating and monitoring
Good Housekeeping Magazine	End-user products evaluation	Reviews, certification, monitoring and warranties
American Automobile Association	Inform travellers about quality of accommodations	Rating and monitoring

incentives to maintain a good credit history. Financial rating agencies help customers make informed investment decisions. A phone call to the local Better Business Bureau in the US or in Canada helps consumers learn more about local businesses. Better Business Bureaus also offer arbitration to customers who are unhappy with their purchases. Consumers Union reviews a wide variety of products and services including spaghetti sauce, vacation spots and managed health care organizations. The Institute of Good Housekeeping extends warranties to products advertised in its magazine.

A majority of these institutions have been providing their services to customers and businesses for a long time. Underwriters' Laboratories, financial rating agencies, and The American Dental Association date back over a century. The Institute of Good Housekeeping was founded in 1901, Consumers Union in 1936. Their long history and large presence prove that 'private regulation' by these market-based institutions is effective.

Even though compliance with the rules and guidelines prepared by these institutions is voluntary, market participants frequently choose to do so, without any statutory mandates or government orders. There is some evidence that firms perceive the compliance costs with privately set rules and guidelines as a necessity for survival in the marketplace rather than as a burden.[7] Furthermore, these institutions have effective enforcement mechanisms. They use legally enforceable contracts with sanctions including revoking of approvals, fines, and pulling products off the market.

Understanding how market based alternatives work may help put the costs and benefits of state regulation in perspective

REGULATION WITHOUT THE STATE notes that most regulations are designed based on some 'ideal model' of the economy, and regulators typically fail to consider the imperfections of the government as a rule-maker and enforcer.[8] Sadly, the same fallacy carries itself into the discussions of regulatory reform. Many

---

[7] For details, see *ibid.*, p. 10.

[8] *Regulation Without the State*, pp. 15–16 (pp. 3–4 of this Readings).

attempts to reform the regulatory system consist of comparisons of the current regulatory agencies with some 'ideal regulatory model.' In fact, state is not the only source of regulation. There is a huge world of market-based institutions, practices and rules and a better understanding of these institutions and practices could allow for comparison of state regulation with an actual model, putting the costs and benefits of the state regulation in perspective.

Understanding how these institutions and practices work are important for a variety of reasons.

- First, market-based alternatives play an important role in promoting good conduct at relatively low costs. As opposed to state regulatory agencies, which are run on tax dollars, market-based standard setters, certifiers and reviewers finance themselves by collecting from the businesses they 'regulate.' Since the price of privately regulated goods reflects the *full cost* of regulation, these institutions are very sensitive to the burdens they impose on businesses and consumers. Market-based institutions not only manage themselves in a cost-effective manner, but also try to lower compliance costs for businesses. In many instances, these institutions eliminate paperwork, and provide businesses with well-formulated guidelines and firm-specific recommendations. Therefore, businesses know the fees and the compliance costs in advance, and can fully assess the expected costs and benefits.

- Second, market-based institutions are flexible and responsive. Standard setting institutions are open to suggestions by industry members, consumers and consumer groups, academic institutions like universities or other scientific organisations, and government agencies. As a result of that dynamic relationship, these institutions closely follow changes and technological advancements to preserve their expert status. They continuously revise their standards or certification procedures.

- Third, the voluntary nature of the market-based alternatives deserves some attention. Private certifiers, rating agencies and reviewers do not directly interfere with the production decision of the sellers and cannot ban low quality producers from selling. There is nothing wrong with a market that supplies low

90

quality goods at low prices; having alternative quality levels sold at 'right' prices increases the variety of our choices. On the other hand, product bans, minimum quality standards and licensing regulations reduce the variety of the products in the market by limiting entry.[9] Furthermore, there may be some buyers who desire goods with quality levels that are below minimum quality standards; others may not be able to afford the high quality product, or may prefer quantity to quality. [10] In these cases, entry restrictions through product bans and licensing become very problematic. In fact by forcing consumers to forgo the regulated good or service, or even buy from the unqualified, the minimum quality standards may end up reducing the quality of the good or the service *received*.[11] Therefore, entry restrictions may result in many distortions, making voluntary private certifications, ratings and reviews viable alternatives.[12]

- Fourth, private institutions set standards, prepare guidelines, and develop measures of quality. When quality information is hard to process, standards and guidelines serve as a reference point or a 'focal point' for the consumers.[13] Various product ratings, or classifications used by independent parties make quality comparisons easier, even when quality information is abundant in the market. By making quality information easier

---

[9] See, for example, Carl Shapiro, 'Premiums to High Quality Products as Returns to Reputation,' *Quarterly Journal of Economics*, Vol. 98, No. 4, 1983, pp. 659–680.

[10] Keith B. Leffler, 'Ambiguous Changes in Product Quality,' *American Economic Review*, Vol. 72, No. 5, 1982, pp. 956–967.

[11] Sydney L. Carroll, and Robert J. Gaston present examples of licensing regulations that result in the reduction of the quality of the service received. For details, see Carroll and Gaston, "Occupational Licensing and the Quality of Service: An Overview," *Law and Human Behavior*, Vol. 7, 1983, pp. 139–146.

[12] This does not mean that market-based institutions deliver "first-best" outcomes or 'socially optimal' standards. However, they supplement the system at a much lower cost. See Kenneth Arrow, *The Limits to Organization*, New York: Norton, 1974, pp. 11–14.

[13] Thomas C. Schelling, *The Strategy of Conflict*, 15th ed., Cambridge, MA and London: Harvard University Press, 1995, pp. 57–59. Also see Schelling's discussion in Thomas C. Schelling, *Micromotives and Macrobehavior*, Norton: New York, 1978.

to understand, intermediaries may reduce the dependence of quality on price.

- Fifth, information problems heavily infest the markets in developing countries.[14] Especially with corrupt public agencies, and problematic government enforcement, market participants generally resort to costly signalling mechanisms as substitutes for quality regulation and enforcement.[15] Introduction of market based alternatives may facilitate good conduct in these markets.

- Finally, understanding how these private institutions operate may help design policies for new or innovative industries with less tolerance to rigid regulation. Examples of markets where private institutions emerged prior to government regulation are the Internet content ratings, organic food markets, and computer hardware and software. Private intermediaries are also developing standards for Internet commerce, electronic cash transfers, environmental friendliness and other areas where property rights are blurred or existing regulations are inadequate. These examples also show that market-based institutions are capable of responding to the changes in the market conditions relatively faster. Therefore understanding how 'private regulation' works may also help develop policies that facilitate competition, and result in less wasteful applications of antitrust regulation.[16]

Conclusions

THE CASE FOR STATE INVOLVEMENT in quality and safety is, at best, weak. The 'market failure' is hard to pin down, and the externalities are commonly misplaced. It is true that there will

---

[14] Eric Durbin, 'McDonald's or Michelin Guide: Revealing Quality Through Private-sector Certification', Unpublished Manuscript, November 1998.

[15] For examples of such signalling mechanisms, see Francis Fukuyama, *Trust: the social virtues and the creation of prosperity*, Free Press: New York, 1995.

[16] For further information, see Horst Albach, Jim Y. Jin, and Christoph Schenk, *Collusion through Information Sharing? New Trends in Competition Policy*, Berlin: Edition Sigma, 1996.

always be some unhealthy or unsafe products in the market. However, as the examples show, markets have developed effective mechanisms to deal with these problems. I believe the state's role in quality and safety regulation must be limited to the support of a sound legal system, which is essential to the operation of market based institutions.

Government: Whose Obedient Servant?

A Primer in Public Choice

Gordon Tullock
Arthur Seldon
Gordon L. Brady

In *Government: Whose Obedient Servant?*, three economists provide an account of the theory of public choice and its applications without the technical jargon which makes it difficult for newcomers to appreciate the importance of this branch of economics.

The authors are three leading exponents. Professor Gordon Tullock is one of the founding fathers of public choice theory and has been responsible for many of the most imaginative ideas and the most significant advances in the subject.
Dr Arthur Seldon, for many years the Editorial Director of the Institute of Economic Affairs, was one of the first to recognise the importance of public choice and has been a principal contributor to the development of the subject in Britain.
Dr Gordon Brady has written extensively about ways in which public choice theory can be applied to some of the most pressing issues of our time.

Sir Antony Jay, joint author of *Yes, Minister* and *Yes, Prime Minister* contributes a Foreword in which he explains how his experiences led him, by a different route, to the same conclusions as those of this 'admirable book'.

The Institute of Economic Affairs
2 Lord North Street, Westminster, London SW1P 3LB
Telephone: 020 7799 3745 Facsimile: 020 7799 2137
E-mail: iea@iea.org.uk Internet: http://www.iea.org.uk   ISBN 0-255 36482-2

£10.00

Overfishing: The Icelandic Solution

Hannes H. Gissurarson

1. Access to Icelandic fisheries was traditionally open to all.

2. In the 1960s and 1970s excessive catches of herring and then cod led to a decline in stocks of these important species in Iceland's waters.

3. In response, Iceland's government imposed restrictions on the number of days trawlers could put to sea to catch certain species.

4. This led to fishing Derbies, where fishermen competed to catch as many fish as possible in the limited time available. Inevitably, catches continued to exceed sustainable levels.

5. Starting in 1979, the Icelandic government gradually introduced a system of individual transferable share quotas (ITQs), which essentially give boat owners the right to catch a specific proportion of the total allowable catch (TAC) of certain species.

6. If a boat owner does not wish to use all his ITQ he can sell part of it to someone else. This encourages more efficient use of the capital invested in boats and equipment.

7. Because ITQs entitle their owners to a specific share of the future stock of fish, they create incentives to ensure that stocks are sustainable.

8. Since the introduction of ITQs, capital invested in Icelandic fisheries (boats and equipment) has been gradually falling and catches have fallen to sustainable levels, whilst the value of catches has risen.

9. Because of the success of the ITQ system and the wealth it has created, there is now political pressure for the imposition of a resource rent tax. But such a tax would be contrary to the interests of effective conservation of fish stocks.

10. A more appropriate next step would be to introduce a cost-recovery charge and, as a *quid pro quo*, give ITQ owners greater say in the administration and enforcement of the system. Owners of ITQ would have stronger incentives to ensure that catch levels were set at the economically optimal level.

The Institute of Economic Affairs

2 Lord North Street, Westminster, London SW1P 3LB
Telephone: 020 7799 3745 Facsimile: 020 7799 2137
E-mail: iea@iea.org.uk Internet: http://www.iea.org.uk   ISBN 0-255 36489-X

£8.00

WHO, What and Why?

Trans-national Government, Legitimacy and the World Health Organisation

Roger Scruton

1. Trans-national institutions (the United Nations and its affiliates) are increasingly exercising their legislative powers, in order to by-pass the constraints to which national legislatures are subject.

2. The situation is made worse by the habit of conferring leadership of these institutions on ex-politicians, rather than experienced civil servants.

3. Such ex-politicians tend to be more responsive to the concerns of vocal but unrepresentative interest groups, who seek to impose their vision on the people of the world.

4. The World Health Organisation (WHO), after years of blatant corruption and abuse, has been put in the hands of Dr Gro Harlem Brundtland, ex-Prime Minister of Norway.

5. The dangers of this are illustrated by the WHO's 'Tobacco Free Initiative', and its current attempt, eagerly pursued by Dr Brundtland, to secure a draconian Convention against the tobacco industry.

6. The grounds given for this are largely spurious, and in any case refer to matters which are outside the remit of the WHO.

7. The effect of the proposals will be to confer massive legislative and policing powers on unaccountable bureaucrats, and also to drive the trade in tobacco underground.

8. The proposed convention will do nothing to curtail the consumption of tobacco, and everything to escalate the criminal activities of smugglers and rogue producers.

9. The time has come for the WHO to concentrate on its real mission, which is the prevention and cure of communicable diseases such as malaria and TB.

10. Only this will answer the legitimate complaints of those who have seen the Organisation squander millions on projects of little or no relevance to Third-World countries.

The Institute of Economic Affairs

2 Lord North Street, Westminster, London SW1P 3LB
Telephone: 020 7799 3745 Facsimile: 020 7799 2137
E-mail: iea@iea.org.uk Internet: http://www.iea.org.uk   ISBN 0-255 36487-3

£8.00